Everything WORTH KNOWING I LEARNED GROWING UP IN FLORIDA

JAY STRACK

WORD PUBLISHING

Dallas·London·Vancouver·Melbourne

Unless otherwise indicated Scripture quotations are from the New King James Version of the Bible. Copyright © 1979, 1980, 1982, Thomas Nelson, Inc., Publishers.

Library of Congress Cataloging-in-Publication Data

Strack, Jay.
   Everything worth knowing I learned growing up in Florida / Jay Strack.
      p.   cm.
   ISBN 0–8499–3514–8 (pbk.)
   1. Success. 2. Florida—Description and travel—Miscellanea.   I. Title.
   BJ1611.2.s773   1993   93–32906
   158'.1—dc20   CIP

Printed in the United States of America

345679 LBM 987654321

Contents

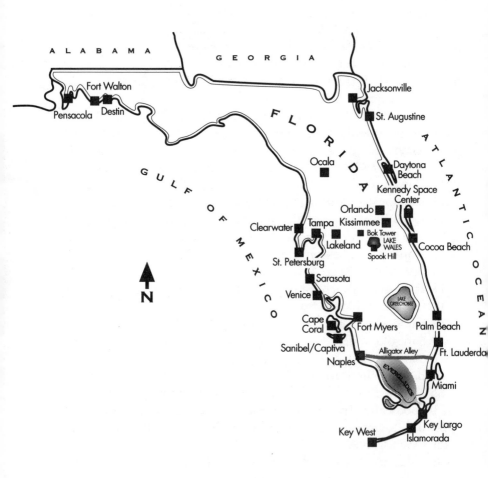

Florida

Foreword

*E*verything Worth Knowing I Learned Growing Up in Florida is truly a unique book by Jay Strack who serves as the tour guide for those who want to really know and enjoy the state of Florida. You'll learn some marvelous things about this beautiful state, its exciting cities, and its outstanding people. And let me quickly add that you'll also learn a lot about life—something all of us are interested in and will benefit from.

Whether Jay is speaking (which he does over two hundred times each year) in an entertaining but powerful, inspiring, and informative way, or writing about the issue of life, he is meticulous, thorough, and humorous. Jay Strack, whose life itself has ranged from the low of the marshlands to the peak of the mountaintop, has the capacity as a writer, speaker, and as a person to take you along on the trip. As you travel with Jay, you will come to know that even in those dark moments that all of us periodically face, he is going to make it. More importantly, you get the feeling that the lessons he's teaching will stand you in good stead and enable you to take your own tour of life that can be just as satisfying and rewarding.

This is a fun book to read; more importantly, it's informative. Even more importantly, it will inspire you to look at your situation, regardless of what it might be, and know that recovery is just a step away. You will just know that there are some things you can do and that regardless of how low you might be, the mountaintops still beckon and are available to those who would climb them. You will come to know that there is still time—and hope—for you. You'll get the feeling that if Jay Strack can overcome his difficulties and challenges, you can do the same thing. What he suggests is practical, down-to-earth, and very workable.

Through it all, Jay's love of life, his family, and his Lord becomes abundantly clear. He delivers a powerful sermon without preaching. Perhaps I see all of these things because I've known Jay for many years. I understand what he's dealt with. I also know he's a man who simply will not quit, and his words and advice come from personal experience and enormous amounts of prayer and research.

Everything Worth Knowing I Learned Growing Up in Florida will give you a better chance to enjoy life on a high note, so pack your bags and join Jay on this tour of life, and I will SEE YOU AT THE TOP!

Zig Ziglar

Introduction

Welcome to Florida! Day after day, people arrive in our sun-drenched, tropical state with all the enthusiasm of the early Spanish settlers. And packed in their luggage are many of the same dreams sought by those first explorers—most notably the vision of a new life. Nicknamed "the Sunshine State," Florida typifies the kind of place that inspired Helen Keller's words, "Keep your face to the sunshine, and you cannot see the shadows."

If you've already arrived in Florida, you have no doubt noticed the swaying palms, southern hospitality, tropical climate, and beautiful beaches. If you're reading this book but not living in or visiting Florida, try to imagine the beauty and put yourself in a "laid-back" frame of mind. Then . . . eat your heart out!

Whether you're planning your trip or already enjoying it, as a native son of the Sunshine State, I think it would be appropriate for me to give you a few words of kindly advice. First of all, true Floridians don't wear plaid shorts with flowered shirts. We don't wear socks with our sandals! And just to be safe, you better give those lily-white legs a few coats of self-tanning cream before you walk around in Bermudas or stretch out in a bikini. And a word of warning: Gators especially love Yankee meat. In case you see them "catching some rays" on many of Florida's fine golf courses, don't get too close. Florida gators wear polo shirts with little *men* embroidered on the chest!

How do I know? I'm what they call a Florida cracker, born and raised here. I grew up with salt water in my veins and sand in my shoes. I love Florida.

What you are about to read is a collection of memories and stories from a lifetime of Florida living. Like shells washed up on the beach, some of my experiences were broken, ugly, and not worth saving; others turned out to be valuable collectibles, treasured and enjoyed again and again.

During my first two decades in Florida, her warm sunshine was overcast by a cloudy and stormy life. The heartache of multiple broken homes, the pain of sexual abuse, and a sense of abandonment led me into a life of drugs and alcohol. I was in trouble with the law numerous times before I graduated from high school. Fortunately, after months of detention, a turning point came for me before it was too late. Since then I have dedicated myself to encouraging others, to sharing positive ideas with them, and to assuring them that *there is hope.*

For the past twenty years, I have spoken face-to-face to more than seven million people in civic clubs, public schools, convention centers, universities, corporate groups, and churches. I enjoy staying behind afterward to listen, laugh, and sometimes share a personal story or two.

No matter where I meet them, people everywhere talk to me about battling the same three issues:

- Overcoming the pain of the past.

- Avoiding mediocrity in the present.

- Finding hope for the future.

In the pages that follow, the colorful history and extravagant variety of Florida's cities serve as a backdrop for some of the life-changing and valuable truths I've gathered along the way. I like to think of the chapters as twenty-first-century parables. Parables (as you might remember from Sunday school) are everyday stories that illustrate important truths. I hope their effect is like an instantaneous flash of lightning against a black sky over the Gulf of Mexico!

Our first lesson, taught by Florida history, was a painful one for Spain. After investing two hundred years of sweat and tears to gain Florida, Spain gave up. Weakened by war, Spain eventually traded away the splendor of Florida in the "tyranny of the moment" for the tiny island of Cuba.

I can relate to this kind of tragedy—I nearly traded my own tomorrows for a temporary haze of alcohol and drug-induced escape from pain. Here's the message I learned from it:

Never sacrifice your future
on the altar of the immediate.

With that perspective as a starting point, I invite you to come along with me through the passionate past and space-age future of Florida. A trip through Florida's romantic history and serene landscape may not reveal Ponce de Leon's fountain of youth. But I can promise you a fountain of truths—truths worth considering, collecting, and counting on for a lifetime.

1 ORLANDO

The Value of Imagination

Like every journey, every book must have a beginning. The first stop on our Florida tour will be Orlando, the heart of the Sunshine State. Besides being a starting point for millions of vacationers each year, Orlando is also the city of my personal beginning. Since I was born in Orlando a few decades ago, the city has continued to hold a special magic for me.

Whether you arrive by plane, train, automobile, or UFO (perhaps the vehicle of choice for those mysterious visitors wearing argyle socks with sandals), in Orlando you will immediately sense a spirit of expectancy in the air.

I remember the Orlando of my boyhood as a lazy, sleepy town of orange groves and cattle ranches. Then one day Mickey and Minnie took up residence smack in the middle of twenty-eight thousand acres of groves and lakes, calling their new home The Magic Kingdom. The place has never been the same since the unique combination of pixie dust, sunshine, and wish-upon-a-star imagination transformed Orlando from the every-day to the enchanted.

In Orlando, I first learned the value of personal vision. Here, names like Disney, Devoss, Amway, Shamu, King Kong, and the Magic and Shaq (the Orlando NBA team and its star player, Shaqile O'Neal) dominate the headlines, dazzle the tourists, and delight the world.

One old adage says,

> ### *Vision*
> ### *is the greatest leadership trait*
> ### *one can possess.*

I believe

> ### *Your dreams determine your destiny.*

There is no place on earth more fitting than Orlando, Florida, to prove both sayings true. Her magic kingdoms offer a kind of contagious vision to all of us.

For years I drove past the same orange groves and pastures for what seemed like a thousand time on my way from our home in Fort Myers to my grandparents' house in St. Cloud. Gradually, the landscape began to change. On each consecutive drive, I noticed fewer trees and more "magic" materializing on the horizon. What seemed incredible, even impossible, at the outset has today evolved into a world-class city.

The story of Walt Disney's humble beginnings and eventual worldwide fame is a fascinating one. He began his career as a cartoonist for the McKinley High School newspaper, and incredibly, that adolescent enterprise shaped his entire future. If he were alive, no doubt he would refer back to that early cartoonist opportunity and say to us,

*What you are doing right now
will affect your tomorrows.*

He would encourage us to give our best to the project at hand, work with all our might, hold on to our dreams, and expect magic kingdoms to open their drawbridges for us. Disney was a slow starter but an avid dreamer. In fact, as a young man his first business attempt ended in bankruptcy.

To me, bankruptcy is not losing your money and assets, it's living without a dream for the future.

I think Disney was always wealthy in heart. When Walt went under financially he immediately moved to Kansas City, where his second enterprise consisted of drawing cartoon strips and advertisements in a small, bare studio. His career never really got off the ground, but the time in K.C. wasn't wasted. It was there that Walt began to make friends with a mouse who ventured out of his hole at night. That mouse, of course, was about to change his life forever.

With the proceeds from the sale of his camera, Walt bought a one-way train ticket to California. In the years to come, he never tired of telling the story of how a certain mouse character was dreamed up on that train trip following his business failure. Disney originally named the mouse Mortimer, but his wife felt the name was too dignified. She suggested "Mickey," and the rest is history.

The most famous imaginary character in the history of the world was actually birthed in disaster!

Many betrayals, rejections, and setbacks followed, but Walt Disney's vision never died. His greatest strength seemed to be the drive that pushed him above and beyond what he had already achieved. He worked. He watched. He listened. He learned from others' successes and failures.

When *The Jazz Singer* debuted as the first talking movie in 1927, Disney latched on to the idea. Without hesitation, he added sound to a cartoon in 1928, creating the first animated film with sound, *Steamboat Willie*. An unparalleled motion picture career was launched. In 1937, he produced the first full-length, color, animated feature, *Snow White and the Seven Dwarfs*, recently re-released on the big screen and still loved by adults and children alike. Before his death in 1966, Disney had produced more than seventy movies.

Just as Mickey Mouse emerged from a dead-end job, Disneyland (Disney World's California predecessor) was dreamed up by a bored father at a kiddie park. Walt was restlessly waiting for his young daughter as she went around and around on a little children's ride. As he sat staring at his mundane surroundings, a vision suddenly began to play in his mind like a motion picture. He imagined a place where parents and children could have fun *together*.

Looking over its development history, a business professor at a major university would surely have declared Walt Disney's dream "Disney's Land of Never Was." During the construction days of Disneyland, the theme park was commonly referred to as "Walt's Folly." However, Disney refused to be deterred. He confidently believed:

> *Any problem can be solved if the*
> *right information can be found.*

Walt was always peering around the next corner, impatiently watching for technology to catch up with his imagination.

> *Don't overlook the everyday as a model*
> *for the possibly spectacular.*

In July 1955, the Disneyland dream became reality. The first sparkling new home of Mickey, Minnie, Goofy, and Donald opened for all the world to enjoy.

Disney drew upon everyday experiences for each new Disneyland idea. For example, Cinderella's castle was conceived from memories of European castles seen during war days. Today, the beguiling castle is said to be the most photographed man-made object in the world.

To be sure Disneyland's beauty was untarnished, Walt used to spend entire nights wandering through the amusement park, personally inspecting benches, flower beds, and walkways for cleanliness. By day, he stood in lines to talk with people and to eavesdrop on their comments. Even though Disney died in 1966, his creativity and his attention to beauty and detail are still imperative in the Disney parks today, which operate in California, Florida, France, and Japan. In Orlando's Disney World alone two million flowers are planted each year.

Disney imagined visions far beyond his own lifetime. This is particularly evident in Epcot Center, where the official literature boasts, "Where else can one venture back to the dawn of recorded history before being propelled to the sunrise of another future? Explore the depths of the ocean, traverse the land, go inside the human body, and race toward the farthest reaches of space." The incredible innovation of Epcot cries out the challenge:

Live in the future tense!

By the time Walt Disney died, he had planted enough seeds of imagination to blossom and bear fruit for many years to come. His dreams did not die with him. Today the Disney Corporation has continued to cultivate, fertilize, and harvest the crops of vision under the capable and dynamic leadership of Michael Eisner.

Volumes have been written in an attempt to unlock and understand the process of imagination, which Walt Disney called "the wellspring of creativity." Personally, I believe each of us has been endowed and engineered by our Creator with the priceless gifts of imagination and creativity. We all possess a magical and mysterious tool more powerful than Aladdin's lamp. We simply need an idea and the belief that dreams can come true.

By now you might be thinking, "Great, Jay, but I'm no Walt Disney." I know the feeling. Neither am I. But I believe all of us can learn to maximize our own imagination. The elements are at our disposal to face and conquer the pressures of today and the challenges of the future.

Disney believed in the wonder of life, and other wise men have shared his perspective. Physicist Michael Faraday once remarked,

> *Nothing*
> *is too wonderful*
> *to be true.*

And Albert Einstein wrote,

> *The most beautiful experience*
> *we have is imagination.*
> *It is a basic emotion*
> *which rocks the cradle*
> *of art, science, and life.*

I have visited Disney's Magic Kingdom, Epcot, and Disney-MGM Studios more than twenty times, read hundreds of articles and books about the Disney phenomenon, and spent hours talking with Disney employees. Through all of my Disney education, I have been making mental notes. These are the lessons Uncle Walt and his colleagues gave me:

- Have a clear vision of what you want. Communicate it effectively to others with word pictures that stir and ignite as they "paint" the story.

- First, see things as they are. Second, feel deeply about the situation. Third, visualize it as you want it to be.

- Utilize the miracle of imagination and vision or you will lose it. Like physical muscles, it only grows stronger with use.

- Build on past experiences, one at a time.

- Never be afraid of change; it almost always brings improvement.

- See the big picture with farsighted vision, and learn to live in the future tense.

- Give full attention to details.

- Speak positively whenever possible.

- If you're going to do it, do it right!

If you've ever wanted inside tips from a successful company, take a look at these statements from the Disney Institute. Before the job even beings, new employees are taught to "Disneyize" their attitudes and careers by

1. Understanding the difference between effective and efficient. Efficient is doing things right. Effective is doing right things right.

2. Choosing the right words:
Challenges, not problems.
New opportunities, not job burnout.
Increased responsibilities, not work overload.

3. Asking themselves, "Am I passive or active?"

4. Asking themselves, "Am I willing to pay a price to make my dreams come true?"

5. Being enthusiastic, even if no one else is—*especially* if no one else is.

Walt Disney was what might be called "a successful failure." A review of his life shows that each failure he encountered played a part in his future success. He coined the phrase *imagineering* to define the process of dreaming the dream and then carrying it out through vision.

Orlando, Florida, reminds us that dreaming doesn't necessarily portray a dissatisfaction with the present. Instead, vision provides avenues for improvement and growth that reach far beyond today, promising all of us better tomorrows.

Every morning, dare to say to yourself, "Just imagine if . . ." And then, with "imagineering," make it happen!

2 ORLANDO

More Magic . . .

It may seem at first that Disney holds a monopoly on the tourist trade in Orlando, but a closer look reveals a pulsating array of attractions that could provide a family with at least a month of vacation excitement. Sea World. Universal Studios. Gatorland. Wet 'n Wild. These and a galaxy of smaller entertainment stars orbit for miles around Orlando.

In the spirit of ongoing entertainment, even Orlando's restaurants are not mere eateries, but evenings of amusement. King Henry's Banquet Feast is a two-hour eighteenth-century production of magic, comedy, and music served alongside a four-course, all-you-can-eat meal.

Next door, the elegant Caruso's Palace will leave you wondering if you didn't actually travel to *Roma* itself. The art, music, food, and ambiance are *belissimo* by any standards.

Don't miss the Hard Rock Cafe. It's on Universal Studios property but is accessible to anyone. Shaped like a guitar and housing an assortment of rock-'n'-roll memorabilia, it is one radical place, and its food is legendary.

Not to be forgotten is the Dixieland Jazz of Rosie O'Grady's Good Time Emporium, aptly and genuinely named. And these are just a few of the food and music establishments that extend throughout the area, covering all tastes—from Bach to bluegrass, from blues to boogie-woogie.

Downtown Orlando doesn't suffer any self-image problems either. By day, it is a flourishing business district; after dark, it throbs with a dazzling diversity of nightlife. One of its most famous stops is the Church Street Station, which features more than fifty shops and restaurants in The Exchange complex.

Orlando's spirit of vision and magic isn't confined to its attractions. Permeating the everyday culture of the city's residents is a contagious zest that is as inspirational as it is incredible. I saw this confirmed when the exciting First Baptist Church of Orlando was proclaimed across the nation by Associated Press and United Press International as a "miracle church" for raising a million dollars in one single offering. The entire country was awed as the congregation sacrificially donated money, wedding rings, cars, and boats to purchase 150 acres and build a six-thousand-seat sanctuary.

This assembly made a bold statement by attempting the impossible by faith. The pastor, Dr. Jim Henry, summarized the miraculous giving: "We believe the people were willing to give because they believe in the vision of attempting great things for God and expecting great things from God."

One visit to the campus of this thriving congregation provides enough motivation to cause even an unbeliever to shout "Hallelujah!"

Perhaps then it is no accident that Pat Williams, presently the general manager of the NBA team known as the Orlando Magic (Is that the perfect name, or what?), can often be seen at this church. In fact, it was while I was spekaing there that I first met this intriguing man with the indefatigable spirit. Pat is known for his enthusiasm, commitment, and personal discipline. But what many don't know is that when Pat and his wife, Jill, along with their twelve children, decided to move to Orlando, the NBA team was merely a simmering notion. There was no facility. The NBA had not yet decided on an expansion team—and it certainly had never so much as mentioned the city of Orlando.

After a successful two-decade career as general manager of the Philadelphia 76ers, the Atlanta Hawks, and the Chicago Bulls, Pat was not about to let such details get in the way of his Orlando dream. One day a chance encounter at the First Presbyterian Church of Orlando led him to ride to the airport with his acquaintance Jimmy Hewitt and Jimmy's friend, John Tolson. As Pat asked about the future of pro basketball in Florida, Hewitt and John unanimously and enthusiastically agreed: "Here! The future of Florida is here!" Pat never expected to hear from them again, but within a few weeks Jimmy Hewitt began calling with excited reports about his progress.

The entire, fascinating story is detailed in *Making Magic*, a book by Pat Williams with Larry Guest, but let me just fill you in on a few of the "opportunities" that lay before them.

Before anything could happen, the NBA had to first agree to expand.

Once that was settled, the NBA set up a rigorous and detailed set of imperatives before they would even consider a city. These included:

• An arena built to the specifications of the NBA. Orlando had none, but an arena *was* on the city's agenda—two years down the road! Intoxicated by the NBA dream, Jimmy Hewitt hired attorneys, put together proposals, and with the help of a lot of friends, assisted in the building of what is now a fifteen-thousand-seat, state-of-the-art showpiece—all done in time for the Magic's opening and according to NBA specs.

• A $32.5 million franchise fee.

• Local radio and TV contracts with a minimum 1.5-million-dollar net revenue for the first season.

- Ten thousand season tickets sold for the 1989-1990 season by December 31, 1988.

Pat Williams was the catalyst for the franchise fee and the media rights, but it was contacts he made through Jimmy Hewitt that caused those things to come about.

As for the ten thousand tickets, however, Williams personally sold thousands of them anywhere he could—at PTA meetings, civic clubs, churches, even in the grocery-store checkout line. He became famous for his relentless persuasion and unabashed publicity seeking that probably caused the Magic to became a reality. Pat refused to give up. He carried on, even when ticket sales were canceled and he had to resell literally thousands of tickets within a short time to avoid losing the expansion award. Even though his persistent, aggressive style was frowned upon by some people, Pat got the job done. As I read in *Making Magic* Pat's account of how the team came about, I discovered some intriguing characteristics of vision and leadership:

1. The vision begins with a *person* who has a picture or an idea firmly entrenched in his or her mind.

2. Through a continued growth *process* the vision stretches, changes, improves, and begins to live.

3. Soon the vision becomes a *panorama* that includes the big picture of possibilities.

4. With *precision*, attention is given to details.

5. Finally the finished *product* emerges.

Once known as "Disney's town," Orlando is now also referred to as the home of the Magic and Shaq—Shaqile O'Neal. When asked how they keep coming up as number one in the draft picks, Williams answers simply and with a smile, "There's magic in Orlando!"

The spirit of Orlando continues to draw great men and women of achievement. Richard Devoss, cofounder of Amway, has moved to Orlando. I have benefited greatly from his books,

Believe! and *Compassionate Capitalism,* and I have adopted many of his insights. When childhood friends Richard Devoss and Jay Van Andel founded Amway, the dream included not only their own success, but support for the dreams of countless others. Their invitation to economic security has been accepted by more than one million men and women throughout the United States and as far away as Japan.

The story began with the development of the first biodegradable soap product. Today Amway's vitamins, cosmetics, and food and household products and the marketing of MCI phone service, water filters, and Coca-Cola machines have made the company the largest door-to-door sales operation in the world. And Amway proves an important principle to be true: *The way to success is paved by enabling others to become successful.*

What is your dream? A vacation home, a new car, a paid-up mortgage, or an exotic vacation . . . ?

What is your career status? Are you holding an unexpected pink slip, waiting for a promotion, stalled in a dead-end job, making the rounds of interviews, or worrying about insufficient retirement funds . . . ?

Whatever your circumstances, Richard Devoss believes Amway can help you. "Most people find very little contentment in the paychecks they receive, so Amway offers more than merely more money. Those who dare to dream and to put feet to their dreams can join an army of motivated, God-fearing, family-centered entrepreneurs," he says.

All of us have dreams, but few of us turn them into reality. How do we get from "imagine if . . ." to "I did it!"? Maybe a simple vocabulary lesson would help:

> *A dream is . . . "just imagine if . . ."*
>
> *A vision is . . . a dream with direction.*
>
> *A goal is . . . a detailed dream with direction and a deadline.*

Keep on going . . . You'll get there!

3 KISSIMMEE

Staying Fresh in Your Vision

When I was a boy, Kissimmee meant the excitement of the Silver Spurs Rodeo. I still remember the excitement—wild horses, daring riders, and a chance to yell my lungs out without getting in trouble.

Back then, Kissimmee was as simple a town as you could hope for, well known as the cattle country and for fresh Florida oranges offering sweet, liquid refreshment at roadside stands. As teenagers, we changed the town's name of Kissimmee to "Kiss-a-me" as we chased the girls and laughed.

In the last twenty years, Kissimmee has bloomed into Orlando's little sister. Today billboards boast of hotels, restaurants, and attractions "just minutes from Disney World." The Crystal City Music Palace promises to be the place "where every night is a Saturday night" as fifties and sixties stars offer rock-'n'-roll background music to your dinner. The Medieval Times Tournament Theatre features jousting knights performing their heroic feats on real horses while patrons feast and cheer from banquet tables. There is plenty to do and see in Kissimmee, and hotel prices are quite competitive.

But even before Orlando began to come to life, another phenomenon was quietly growing on an eleven-hundred-acre site among the cabbage palms and pastures in nearby Kissimmee. About forty years ago, a revolution was launched by a company we all know now as a household word: Tupperware. What home would dare be without it? Last year,

- Eighty-seven million people attended at least one Tupperware party.

- There was a Tupperware demonstration in full swing somewhere in the world every 2.7 seconds.

- Ninety percent of all American homes had at least one Tupperware product.

Earl Tupper's story is pure Cinderella in theme. His family was poor, and he was mostly self-educated. An inventor at heart, Tupper worked in a DuPont chemical plant where he met his responsibilities efficiently. However, he wasn't satisfied with his day-to-day duties. After leaving Dupont, his hunger for new knowledge inspired him to begin a series of experiments. The only available material he had to work with was the chunks of waste left behind in the oil refining process, which his former employer was willing to sell him. This waste was called polyethylene slag—a substance that was black, putrid, hard, and as impossible to work with as rock.

Polyethylene slag isn't much to begin with, unless you use the magic wand of vision on it as Earl Tupper did. Just as Cinderella's fairy godmother turned pumpkins and mice into something useful and glorious, Tupper took something worthless and made it a necessity. After learning on his own how to purify the nasty substance, he discovered ways to mold the resulting product into practical household products. Why hadn't someone else come up with such an idea? For one thing, no one else could see the potential in polyethylene slag. Tupper had to create both a refining process and an injection molding machine. In other words, he literally started from scratch.

Maybe no one ever told him it couldn't be done—because he did it. I guess no one ever said, "It won't work, Earl. It's useless junk!" because he turned his slag into a billion-dollar industry. Or maybe . . .

Earl Tupper just refused to listen.

Creating products was only the beginning. Next Tupper adopted marketing strategies to guarantee the success of his invention. One secret to Tupper's success was seeing a need that no one else noticed and then filling it. He saw that in his time almost anyone could buy a refrigerator or freezer, but no one knew how to keep refrigerated food fresh or how to prevent containers from breaking when used over and over again.

Tupper *was* listening when people talked about those kinds of needs. From idle conversations, he brainstormed the development of his original product line. Next, he put his marketing scheme to work. Like Mary Kay and other pioneer marketers, Tupper recognized the enormous potential of putting homemakers in sales, for women were eager to earn extra income without leaving the children all day every day. He hired a woman named Brownie Wise to create the home-party and set up the direct-selling system that is synonymous with Tupperware today.

Brownie's plan was twofold:

• Motivate and inspire dealers to excel.

• Create an atmosphere of fun and excitement for customers.

She introduced a new way of life to thousands of housewives. She taught them how to sell, and she enabled them to make money on their own without taking a nine-to-five job outside the home. Women loved the concept, and years later they still do.

So how does a product that began with primitive refrigeration continue its success through forty years of innovation?

Tupperware not only tells the world how to keep food fresh by using its products, the company also serves as a role model with a few tricks about keeping a business fresh. For example:

- Add new products to fill the changing needs of the consumer.

- Continually update or delete current products.

As food and kitchens became mobile, so did Tupperware. Furthermore, when microwave cooking was added to conventional preparation, the TupperWave stack cooking system came along to meet the needs of today's hectic family schedules.

And how about enabling company personnel to "stay fresh"? This is how they do it:

**Build the people and
the people will build the business.**

This is a guiding principle for the sales force.

Tupperware's all-American success story began because a man named Earl Tupper refused to settle for a routine job and rejected the belief that you can't begin with nothing. He kept on pushing to learn and to grow, to invent and discover.

**Start with what you have.
Find a way to make it better.**

The poet Longfellow was once asked the secret of his continued and consuming interest in life. He pointed to an apple tree and said, *"The purpose of that tree is to grow a little new wood each year. That is what I plan to do."*

In the twenty-first century, the commitment to "staying fresh" is not a luxury; it is a necessity. The rate at which knowledge is exploding around us is astounding. We are being drawn irresistibly by the super-magnet of the new millennium.

The year 1500 marks the beginning of what is known as the "modern era." It took more than three centuries, from 1500 to 1830, for the amount of available scientific knowledge to double.

It doubled again from 1830 to 1930.
It doubled again from 1930 to 1960.
It doubled again from 1960 to 1975.
It doubled again from 1975 to 1985.

Currently, it is predicted that available scientific knowledge will double about every five years. Each year forty-five thousand new book titles are published in English, and more than fifteen hundred journals and magazines are available to the general public. Just when we think we know something, along comes the tenth edition of Merriam-Webster's Collegiate Dictionary with ten thousand new entries. Even "ain't" ain't considered improper anymore!

Staying fresh in our vision requires us to constantly re-evaluate each area of our lives, making changes and improvements as we see the need. We do this not because we are inferior or weak but because we can always be better in the everyday lives on our way to the future. My favorite definition of insanity is

*Doing the same thing the same way
and expecting different results.*

At one time or another, most of us feel as though our life, our career, or our family life is in a rut. Zig Ziglar says,

*A rut is a grave
with both ends knocked out.*

Moving forward in life is a choice—a simple decision. You'll be the same person five years from now except for the books you read, the places you go, and the people you meet.

If we're going to be dissatisfied with any part of our lives, let's be dissatisfied with the amount of knowledge we have. As Daniel Boorstin once said,

*The greatest obstacle to discovery
is not ignorance.
It is the illusion of knowledge.*

There is always something *fresh* to learn, to discover, to conquer. Think about the possibilities. Then, as the ads say, "Just do it!" Read the Bible through. Take a computer or language class. Make the trip you've always dreamed about. Find ways to meet new people. Never, never stop growing!

Look at it this way: If we make this commitment to staying fresh, we will have the same "lifetime guarantee" Tupperware offers. You can't get much more successful than that!

4 DAYTONA BEACH

Start Your Engines!

One of my earliest childhood memories is hearing the words, "Jay, be careful!" I was always on the edge of falling into a disaster. This counsel has echoed throughout the course of my life, always spoken by well-intentioned family members and friends. The words may have been rearranged a bit at times, but they always meant the same thing: Play it safe . . . Don't take foolish chances . . . Take it easy . . . Go nice and slow.

As a kid, I smiled at this kind of advice, but it didn't really sink in. I guess there's always been a passion within me to do something daring. Like other energetic young men and women, I always wanted to break away from the mediocre. In Daytona Beach I first witnessed a spirit of freedom and daring that made me all but burst with excitement.

One of America's most popular resort areas, Daytona's name is synonymous with sun, sand, surf, and speed. Since the early 1900s people have ventured here in search of action. Most of them have heard of the spectacular twenty-three-mile stretch of white-sand beach sparkling with the promise of adventure. The sand is made smooth by the constant flow tides and is packed so hard you can drive a car on it. Believe it or not, it's just like in the movies!

Here, in 1903, Alexander Winston broke the world automobile speed record by driving over sixty-eight miles per hour. (Most of us "break" the speed limit on the freeway at about the same rate of speed, but when we're "written up" it's with a scowl instead of a cheer!) Ever since then enthusiasts have flocked to the Daytona raceway. In 1959, the glamour of the beach began to play second fiddle to the sizzle of the Daytona International Speedway. Racing greats Fireball Roberts, Richard Petty, Mario Andretti, Cale Yarborough, A. J. Foyt, Bill Elliott, and Darrell Waltrip came to race here. And from around the globe, hundreds of thousands of spectators still find their way to Daytona to hear the announcement "Gentlemen [and recently they added ladies], start your engines."

Elaborate, finely tuned autos and cycles speed around the 2.5-mile oval track against a backdrop of cheering fans and thundering engines. Vicarious racing thrills are experienced by spectators in the stands as they watch those who dare to conquer speed and power. The men and women who drive those vehicles have not only dreamed their dream of speed, competition, and excellence, they have turned it into reality.

Like life, the Daytona races separate people into two main groups: those who are watching from the stands and those in the driver's seat, ready to compete in the race. Ever think about which group you are in?

Even though I like to think of myself as a driver rather than a spectator, I know there are times when stress and challenges move me into neutral gear. I tend to "rev" my engine for a while and sometimes "stall out." My gears freeze up, and I'm stuck at the starting line. I find myself saying, "It's too difficult right now. I just don't have time anyway. Maybe next year."

With all the inner stamina I can find, I force myself to replace these words with:

Today is the day to move off the starting line.
The future starts now!

More fuel is injected into my brain as I repeat the words of Fulton Oursler:

> *We crucify our today between two thieves:*
> *regret for yesterday*
> *and fear of tomorrow.*

If I'm still feeling hesitant, I turn to biographies of people I admire, or I read modern-day, extraordinary stories of accomplishment. After all, if they can do it, so can I!

Then I make the conscious decision to move forward. I am now ready to put it in gear, accelerate, and head into the race.

Just as the drivers need mechanical and refueling pit stops, I often find myself in need of mental "pit stops." Reading the incredible stories of victory recorded in the pages of the Bible also sends my spirit soaring. Listening to a variety of speakers on tape keeps my mind primed to think positively and creatively while focusing on the finish line ahead. Picking up the latest copy of *Success* magazine is like high-octane fuel.

Try some of these for yourself:

Be known as a person who gets things done. Henry Ford said,

> *You can't build a reputation*
> *on what you are going to do.*

There is always a way to make things work. Consider this Chinese proverb:

> *The man who says*
> *it can't be done*
> *should not stand in the way*
> *of the man doing it.*

Work for the satisfaction of doing the job well. Andy Granatelli became famous doing just that. He said,

> *When you are making a success*
> *of something, it is not work. It is a way of*
> *life you actually enjoy because you are*
> *making a contribution.*

Pursue opportunities realistically, one accomplishment and one obstacle at a time. As a Hindu sage once observed,

> *Anyone can eat an elephant*
> *a bite at a time.*

Start moving, and don't stop until you cross the finish line. Charles F. Kettering had some worthwhile wisdom for all of us, no matter what we're trying to accomplish. He said:

> *Get started and keep going. By doing so*
> *the chances are you will stumble on*
> *something, often when you are least*
> *expecting it.*
> *I have never heard of someone stumbling*
> *on something sitting down.*

All of these steps work together to encourage me in believing success is just around the next curve.

The race is on. Gentlemen, ladies—start your engines! And, by the way, don't listen to that well-intentioned warning to "take it easy." Give it all you've got. Go for the win!

23

5 KENNEDY SPACE CENTER

Keep Reaching for the Stars

Whenever I drive through the Kennedy Space Center, I am immediately transported into fantasy. For the moment, I imagine that I am an astronaut exploring new frontiers and destined to go "where no man has gone before."

While you're in Florida, Kennedy Space Center is a destination you won't want to miss. Rocket prototypes stand majestically in view, and at nearby Spaceport USA the IMAX theater is guaranteed to almost put you into orbit.

One day I was privileged to enjoy a VIP tour of the compound. Staring at the launch pad, I could only try to envision the hours and years of research, sweat, and tears that created the accomplishment of the impossible. Later, I surveyed the rows

and rows of plaques commemorating the success of each consecutive launch. I couldn't help but notice the one blank spot,
left empty in memory of the *Challenger* launch.

I suppose everyone recalls that sorrowful day in 1986
when the courageous star of discovery and exploration tragi-
cally fell from the sky. The story that follows was related to me
by Gene Thomas, launch director for the 1986 *Challenger* shuttle.
Today he serves as the deputy director of the NASA Kennedy
Space Center.

The morning of January 28, 1986, was a bitter cold and
clear day along the Florida coast. *Challenger* had been
checked and rechecked to make it ready for the long-
awaited launch. The "go- no-go" poll was conducted
around the globe and each confirmed: "It's a go!" A serene
voice contrasted with the incredible setting of power as
each major milestone was announced and thousands of
mechanical and electronic wonders confirmed their net-
working link between the shuttle and the ground equipment. Exuberance filled the air as each indicator turned
green, affirming the expectation of success.

Coming out of the hold at T-minus-nine minutes, the
tension continued to build as computers began the schedule of consecutive moves toward a launch, a reach for the
stars. The *Challenger* countdown continued as we again
polled the same engineers and managers to get the final
go-ahead to pick up the count. The decision to launch *Challenger* on that freezing day was not taken lightly. Hundreds
of managers, engineers, and technicians had worked
throughout the night to analyze data and make the decisions concerning the temperature.

The clock reached the crucial T-minus-thirty-one-
seconds point and the on-board computers responded by
taking charge of the launch to control all critical functions
on the shuttle. At T-minus-ten seconds, giant sparklers ignited; at T-minus-six seconds, the three main engines
started sequentially and the signal was relayed to fire the

solid rocket motors. Excitement and anticipation were thick enough to stand on.

The count of T-minus-zero brought the final ignition and liftoff. An immense pillow of brilliant white smoke seemed to easily lift the four and one-half million pounds of machinery into the clear, blue Florida sky. Shouts of joy abounded as the firing room vibrated from the powerful launch and overwhelming tears rolled shamelessly down faces. Triumph filled the room as the T-plus countdown rolled on.

The Launch Team sat in silent anticipation of separation of the rocket from the boosters.

Then, in a split second, smiles faded and faces froze in horror as the count reached T-plus-seventy-three seconds and *Challenger* burst into flames. Immediately, terror overtook all of us as we watched the once powerfully majestic *Challenger* burn and fall helplessly into the ocean, drowning the hopes and futures of our friends.

My first hope was that *Challenger* could sail clear of the fireball and circle back to a glide onto the Kennedy Space Center landing facility. Then the awful truth became apparent to me. My technical mind overcame the desires of my heart as I soberly dealt with the facts: *It can't separate during first stage; everyone in the orbiter will be destroyed.*

There was absolutely no hope! I sat in my chair, stunned and in shock. Eerie silence dominated the room as disbelief paralyzed each of us. There had been no warning to anyone of impending danger—no malfunctions, no obvious failure trends, no data anomalies. We had worked so valiantly to lift her, and she had responded by crushing us in her fall.

I sat in shock, prayed for some miracle to save the crew, and literally fought back the tears. I felt nauseated from thoughts of the trauma my astronaut friends must have suffered. Then a peace pervaded my heart, and I heard these words, *son, you are not to worry for I am still in control.* My faith bolstered me in the next few hour of confusion.

Almost at once we were faced with the task of defining

the cause of explosion, a task requiring us to watch the tragedy over and over again by video. I had prayed, sweated, lived, and breathed this wondrous adventure into space. Now it played before me like a horror movie. Some twenty hours later, I finally drove home, not remembering how I got there.

My body shook as I wrung my hands and clung to my dear loved ones. Together we wept as my whole being cried out for understanding, but there was none. This monumental catastrophe could be traced back to my final words: "It's a go." They rang in my ears until utter exhaustion finally drove them out.

I awoke the next morning with the hope that the whole disaster had been a bad dream, but reality quickly set in. I made my way to work, where I remember giving a short speech about getting some answers and pressing on with the shuttle program. In my own heart, I had already lost a lot of spirit, and I had to swallow hard to keep the words "I quit!" from escaping my throat.

For days and weeks afterward, I went through the motions, but numbness had overtaken me. I thought I might be asked to resign, but it didn't seem to matter. Human error had killed my friends. I had loved these men and women, and they had depended on me to assure their safety and success. I had encouraged each of them to reach for the stars. Now the stars were falling and with them the weight of the world fell on me.

Day after day I could hear the explosion in my mind, taunting me. This went on for weeks and months until one day I realized another vision was slowly overtaking my mind. I cannot say exactly what it was that prompted my healing. Perhaps I was fueled by my desire to make some sense of the tragedy and to know that my friends had not died in vain. I vividly remember the day when, staring out those vast picture windows at the launch pad, an inner strength flowed through my being.

Again I saw the vision of a launch, and this time I knew it would be successful.

As I listened to Gene Thomas, I fought back tears of my own. It was painfully apparent that of all the lessons I had ever learned in Florida, I was about to receive one of the most beneficial:

Keep reaching for the stars AFTER a tragedy.

Throughout my life, I have known many people who have allowed adversity to bury them in despair. Having survived their personal crises, they are afraid ever to dream again. In my visit with Gene Thomas, four steps emerged as he described his personal healing process:

Faith. The words of encouragement from God speaking into his heart combated the taunting voice of disaster. These positive words won out and gave Gene the strength to press on. Every Sunday Gene attends church, grateful for the encouragement he receives through the hymns and the Bible. Gene says his faith in the Lord gave him what he needed to survive not only in the midst of that one, dark storm, but to succeed in day-to-day stresses of life.

Family. Moments after the disaster, Gene's son Chuck was on the phone. He had heard of the accident while attending class at Palm Beach Atlantic College.

"Dad," he said, "God told me to tell you He is still in control."

Gene felt instant comfort in Chuck's words as he realized they matched his own experience. And, coming home dazed, Gene fell into the waiting arms of his wife, Juanita, and daughters, Karen and Wendy. The love of family is a comfort like no other.

Friends. Visiting the Kennedy Space Center is like walking in on a family business. Never before have I been to a place where there is such respect and pride in speaking of fellow workers, from the administration to the hands-on mechanics. Everyone fully believes in the importance of relying on one another. Each consecutive action networks with the next action to move toward the final accomplishment.

That fateful day in 1986 the closest friends of Gene Thomas were those working alongside him. Together they picked up the pieces and carried one another through.

Future. Hope is the final summation: "We will be better. We will launch again." Gradually, Gene and those involved regained their confidence in the future. They had to, not only out of respect for the Challenger Seven and the preservation of their dreams, but for the sake of those who would follow in their steps.

Abraham Lincoln once said:

> *The best thing about the future*
> *is that it comes*
> *one day at a time.*

I believe it is faith in the future that fuels us to perform in the present. I think Gene agrees with me, as you'll see in the conclusion to his story:

> Months and months of reviews and inspections extended into what is now commonplace safety procedure. NASA will never again be accused of laxity or oversight. Critical self-evaluations brought about a revitalization of safety and an improvement in priority.
>
> Today, many years later, the pain remains deeply etched into my soul. I shall never forget that day; nor do I want to. Sometime after the *Challenger* incident, my secretary, Barbara, delivered a gift to me. It was a picture of the *Challenger* crew, signed by each one, with these words: "To the greatest launch director in the world."
>
> I know now that I operated correctly based on the information given, and they would have agreed with me. I shall always cherish their thoughts of me, and I have prominently displayed the photo in my den where I see it often. It is a reminder of the thousands of stars beckoning me to reach for them.

As awesome as the sight of a falling star can be, I know there are still myriads of twinkling lights faithfully shining in their place in the sky.

Stars don't come with a guarantee. I know the storm must pass before I can get a clear view of them.

Looking at the photo of my good friend Dick Scobee, I hear him say, "Gene, never, *never* stop reaching for those stars."

I am sure he is looking down at me as I reply, "We never will, Dick. We never will."

6 COCOA BEACH

Surf's Up, Dude!

Ask anyone about Cocoa Beach, and they're sure to tell you about two things: great surf and the spectacular Ron Jon's Surf Shop. Known for its signature "One of a Kind" slogan, the retail store has a unique story behind its phenomenal growth. Founder Ron DiMenna started with three surfboards in New Jersey in early 1960, using his father's deli as a storefront. Three years later, he left New Jersey for Florida with a truck and six hundred dollars' worth of merchandise, settling in Cocoa Beach where a small surfing crowd was beginning to form. His original three-thousand-square-foot store has exploded into a fifty-two-thousand-square-foot surfing attraction, deserving a tour whether you surf or not. Open twenty-four hours a day, 365 days a year, Ron Jon's has sold more than sixteen million T-shirts, offers a complete line of water-sports equipment, and even contains its own post office. It is particularly spectacular at night when the cathode lighting adorning the deco facade can be seen from five miles away. Ron Jon's is a long way from that New Jersey deli!

One thing's for sure: When the surf's up at Cocoa, you better get out of the way unless you're surfacing because surfboards suddenly take claim over the waves. There's a certain thrill to conquering these unstable rides that causes young and old alike to go back again and again, no matter how many times the waves throw you off. I remember as a fifteen-year-old teen begging my mom, "I've got to have a new surfboard for my birthday. And it *has* to be from Ron Jon's Surf Shop. I'll do anything! Please!"

So there I was, soaked and salty, astride my new board, with those pleading words playing and replaying in my mind. I heard them every time another wave knocked me over and the board hit me on the head.

Why did I ever want this surfboard, anyway? I wondered, rubbing my head. *Why not something safer—like a pet alligator or a motorcycle?* Not only was I feeling intense pain, but my ego was suffering a series of major setbacks as the ocean got the best of me, wave after wave.

Paddling in for a rest, I sat on the sand and watched the other surfers. Could I learn something from them that would save me some suffering? Trying my best not to look exhausted, I grinned bravely at every girl who walked by. I tried to appear nonchalant, as though I had simply chosen to soak up some rays.

When I wasn't catching my breath or rubbing my head, I was asking myself a vital question about the other surfers. *How do they do that? They get up, and they ride the wave until it dies. I get up, and I wait for it to kill me.*

Just then one of the better surfers came out of the water and sat beside me. I couldn't hold back the question: "Who taught you to surf like that?"

I was hoping for a formula, but all he said was, "I did. Every time the wave throws you, just get back on. Pretty soon, you learn the different kinds of waves, and you've got it. Grab the board, get back on it, and don't give up."

Easy enough for you to say, I thought. After all, he wasn't suffering a pounding headache and a black-and-blue body. Still, what he'd said made sense. *Hmmm, learn the different kinds of waves. Maybe he's got something there.*

I began to study the waves as though they were review material for a final exam in physical science. I soon learned how to tell them apart, and then I put them in categories.

Low, steady swell. This is the safest ride. You won't ride high on this kind of wave, but it will surely take you into shore. It's like the sure bet in life, and a majority of waves fall into this category. While they won't offer you much in the way of excitement, they are an honorable and bona fide ride.

Sudden crest. A quick burst of intensity makes this a short ride. Just as quickly as the wave picks up the board, it drops you flat, crashing within seconds and tossing you off balance. It's the "shortcut" to the top that never really gets you there.

Faraway visibility. Here is deception flowing right at you. You wait with anticipation, but the wave crashes before it ever gets to you, dashing your hopes and dreams of "the big one." This wave usually carries with it a sense of apathy and discourages you from trying again. Don't leave the beach just yet; another wave of opportunity will follow shortly.

Appearance of perfection. The greatest dare comes at you with a false offer of perfection. Expecting no problems, you are suddenly challenged with the ferocity of a powerful current. It takes all the fancy dancing and footwork you can muster just to stay on the board, but in the end it's a thrilling victory. Reaching the goal is worth the sweat.

The long ride. Well worth paddling surf all day for, you can climb aboard and your expectations are fulfilled in a sensational ride. It takes hours of waiting and a variety of experiences in between before you get this shot, but it does come. The key is to keep on paddling, all the while anticipating success.

Having made my observations, I swam out into the ocean, ready to try again with my newfound wisdom. I was intent on the victory—me against the surf. One thing was obvious: The next wave would be coming at me, whether or not I was ready for it! I stared at those mountains of water, and they stared back. The roar of the surf chanted a dare as though we were boxers sparring in a ring: *Get up! Get back up again, you coward!*

We wrestled for hours. I soon found that the only way of winning was to keep getting back on the board for the next try, no matter how impossible it seemed.

It certainly doesn't take a philosopher to see the similarities between my teenage discoveries about surfing and some grownup truths about life. Almost every day, the decision stands before us. We can be detoured by personal failures and slow starts, or we can get up and keep going. Anyone can be successful in spite of past or present downfalls—or even perhaps because of them.

Maybe you've noticed that most of those we view as highly successful have either begun with a small start or have endured numerous failures. History gives us insight into many other "successful failures."

Ty Cobb was thrown out more times trying to steal bases than any man in baseball history. Yet for more than half a century he was the career base-stealing leader and is described as baseball's fiercest competitor.

Babe Ruth struck out more times than any other man in baseball history. Today he is remembered as the best player of all time. He was the first player to hit 30, 40, 50, and finally 60 home runs in a single season. His home-run record of 60 and his career home-run total of 714 stood for decades.

Hank Aaron, who broke Ruth's record, struck out more times than 99 percent of those players who make it to the major leagues. But his career averaged thirty-three home runs a year, and he was named an All Star each of the twenty-three seasons he played.

Nobody on the planet considers these individuals failures, and only trivia buffs even remember their unsuccessful attempts. Here are some more inspiring examples of successful failures:

Enrico Caruso's voice failed to carry the high note so many times that his voice teacher advised him to quit. He kept on singing and today is recognized as one of the greatest tenors ever to live.

Thomas Edison's teacher called him a dunce and labeled him as "addled." I don't have to tell you of his apparent genius.

Albert Einstein flunked a course in math and was labeled slow by some of his teachers (an obvious error by some very embarrassed educators!).

In 1955 Johnny Unitas failed his first pro test with the Pittsburgh Steelers. The first time he took over in a game, he fumbled three times, and each of those fumbles resulted in a touchdown for the opposing team. But in 1970, during the commemoration of the fifty-year anniversary of the National Football League, Johnny Unitas was selected as the greatest quarterback of all time.

Henry Ford was flat broke at age forty. No wonder he once said,

> *Failure is an opportunity*
> *to begin again*
> *more intelligently.*

You and I must realize that it is OK to fail.

> *Failing in one particular effort doesn't*
> *mean you are a failure as a person.*

Often I meet people who reside on "Alibi Alley." They have a built-in excuse and a rationale for all their woes, explaining why others can succeed but they cannot and bemoaning the reasons why they've given up. How can they forget so many current heroes who, when knocked down, refused to stay down?

Mario Lemieux of the National Hockey League's Pittsburgh Penguins has battled both back injuries and Hodgkin's disease, a type of cancer. Is it any wonder he is considered one of the greatest hockey players ever to play? I believe his attitude holds the secret to his tenacity. He says, regarding his cancer, "I have faced a lot of battles since I was very young, and I have always come out on top. I expect that will be the case with this disease."

Sally Jesse Raphael, the well-known talk-show host, told *Parade* magazine about her difficult journey. After graduating from the Columbia School of Broadcasting with A's, the only female in her graduating class, she was told by the dean, "You haven't been hired by anyone because you are the wrong sex."

In 1963, she found herself divorced with two daughters. Her father had passed away, and her career was going nowhere. After years of news, traffic, and weather, she could not even find a sponsor. She moved from job to job, never giving up, always learning from her mistakes.

Sally's big break came on October 7, 1983, when the Sally Jesse Raphael show premiered out of Saint Louis. Today it airs in more than two hundred markets in the United States and in five other countries. And this lady, who once lived in her car, makes more than a million dollars a year. I have had the privilege of being on her show twice, and I can tell you, Sally is a genuinely nice, hard-working woman.

Theodore Seuss Geisell, born in 1904 in Springfield, Massachusetts, hardly seemed destined for greatness. His high school art teacher discouraged him, saying, "You will never learn to draw." His Dartmouth College fraternity voted him least like likely to succeed, and he dropped out of Oxford, bored and restless.

Geisell's first job as a cartoonist was for a magazine so close to bankruptcy that he got paid in cases of shaving cream and soft drinks. Twenty-seven publishers rejected his manuscripts. They said the stories were silly and the rhymes nonsensical.

Finally an editor agreed to take a chance, and "Dr. Seuss" was born. He worked a year and a half to write *The Cat in the Hat*, which sold half a million copies during 1957, its first year in print. He left a legacy of optimism and enthusiasm, and when he died more than 210 million copies of his books had been purchased.

Bo Jackson, a super athlete, battled back from an injury that knocked him out of both football and baseball. He never quit; he overcame all the odds and hit a home run in his first game after returning to the Chicago White Sox.

Soichino Honda, founder of Honda Motors, observed,

Many people dream of success. To me, success can be achieved only through repeated failure and introspection. In fact, success represents only 1 percent of your work that results from 90 percent of that which is called failure. Very few unacquainted with failure will know the joy of true success.

You'll probably see bumper stickers around Florida that say "Life's a Beach." Maybe it's true. The lessons I learned surfing at Cocoa Beach continue to motivate me today:

*If you're knocked off your surfboard,
get back on!
Failure isn't fatal unless you label it as final.*

7 PALM BEACH

In Search of Excellence

The moment you enter Palm Beach, the fantasy of paradise on earth seems fulfilled. Glittering shops, swaying palms, and an air of luxury abound throughout this lovely resort city. It's hard to imagine such a place beginning as a simple, undeveloped sand key, but that's exactly what it once was. Palm Beach is a Shangri-la of the most humble beginnings.

History tells us about a Spanish boat that shipwrecked off the island centuries ago, leaving behind a cargo of coconuts. They washed ashore, took root in the sand, and eventually transformed the barren terrain into a tropical Eden.

Interestingly, the pattern of the humble evolving into the fabulous has occurred again and again in the story of Palm

Beach, most notably in the story of the luxurious and palatial Breakers Hotel, originally built by Henry Morrison Flagler. Don't dare visit Palm Beach without strolling the gardens, gawking over the priceless artwork, and reading the story of the hotel's visionary beginnings. It's a temporary indulgence you won't forget!

Some years ago, I'd met Emelio, reservations manager for the hotel, at the First Baptist Church of West Palm Beach when I spoke at their enchanting Chapel by the Sea. So when the time came for our adventure at The Breakers, I called him and said, "Fix me up, Emelio; I'm coming over to see you." Soon we were on our way.

The palm-lined entrance of The Breakers lured us inside with its promise of extravagance and luxury. I parked our compact rental car as gracefully as I could next to the rows of Rolls-Royces, Mercedes, and other luxury autos and proceeded inside. Instantly I forgot my tiny rented car and my beat-up luggage as I was transported into the atmosphere of wealth, excellence, and prosperity—at least for the moment!

Walking through the lobby, I felt like Alice opening the door into Wonderland. The grandeur and splendor of the interior is reminiscent of the Italian Renaissance, and for a moment I thought I had been transported to a European palace. We wandered from hallway to hallway, savoring every area. Gold-leaf ceilings, elaborate carpets, rare antique tapestries, and incredible, crystal chandeliers filled room after room.

How did Henry Flagler put together such magnificence? I wondered to myself.

It was Sunday around noon, so after checking in we found our way into the dining room for a bite of lunch. At first I thought we had intruded on a celebrity wedding or some grand social event of the season, but I soon discovered that this Sunday brunch was available to the public—for a price, of course. Ice sculptures and food too pretty to touch abounded at every turn. An air of elegance permeated the dining areas. Celebrities were such a common sight that hardly anyone seemed to notice (except for Diane and me!).

After brunch, Emelio showed us to our private cabana by the beach. *This is the life,* I thought, *a private waiter, an extra-thick chaise lounge, fluffy towels, our own shower, and a panoramic view of the ocean!*

As the day went by, I thought perhaps I should ask Emelio if we could live right here next to the sea forever. Unfortunately, however, all good things must come to an end.

As we were leaving, I took time to study and appreciate the myriad works of art displayed throughout the world-famous Breakers. Portraits of the rulers and explorers of the New World were fascinating. But it was the panel over the great stone fireplace that really captured my imagination.

I stood transfixed by the depiction of the New World boldly emerging from the clouds of the Old World. The scene lingered in my mind.

Later on I read a booklet explaining the origin and history of The Breakers. Suddenly it occurred to me that the Old World/New World development wasn't just ancient history. It was at the heart of Flagler's bold vision for a haven of luxury on the east coast of Florida. His quest to create something extraordinary was fulfilled as the "New World" of Palm Beach emerged from a palm-forested sand key.

During my wonderfully restful and intriguingly interesting stay, I collected these souvenirs of Flagler's success formula:

It's all in how you see it. Henry Flagler, at the age of sixty-three, contemplated the undeveloped beauty of Palm Beach. It was in a remote location, and no transportation linked it to well-traveled cities. Nevertheless, Flagler saw the obstacles as immense opportunities. In his mind this vast, private emptiness with the world's greatest view of the Atlantic would be an idyllic spot for a luxury tourist haven.

Turn obstacles into opportunities. Recognizing the beauty of the seaside area, Flagler didn't wait for the transportation situation to improve. He created his own Florida East Coast Railway to bring the guests into town.

Flagler viewed the absence of bridges linking Palm Beach to nearby West Palm Beach or other nearby establishments as an asset, not a drawback. This kept all visible business enterprise away from Palm Beach, marking it as an exclusive, secluded resort. **Keep the big picture in mind.** Flagler, the entrepreneur, refused to shortcut any part of his dream. Not only did he begin construction on the largest hotel in Florida in 1893, but he also envisioned it as a world-renowned resort and mapped out a city to surround it. Almost overnight the Royal Poinciana Hotel and the Palm Beach Inn became successful and were expanded. Among the wonders that drew curious travelers was a one-thousand-foot pier called the Port of Palm Beach.

A good reputation breeds success. Flagler's "palace by the sea" began a tradition of hosting elegant charity balls. This attracted society leaders and celebrities from all over the world. Suddenly this pearl beside the ocean was *the* place to be and to be seen. Prominent families reserved the oceanfront cottages as winter homes. Frequent guests such as John D. Rockefeller, President Warren G. Harding, William Randolph Hearst, the Duchess of Marlborough, and Andrew Carnegie added to the mystique of The Breakers as word spread of its world-class status.

Enable others to thrive through your accomplishments. Henry Flagler's railroad was the catalyst for the development of other industries, cities, and resorts from Saint Augustine to Key West. Meanwhile, like lesser stars surrounding a beautiful constellation, mansions began to rise up around The Breakers. One architect, Addison Mizner, caught the Palm Beach vision. He designed and crafted the Spanish style of architecture that still represents the opulence of the 1920s. In the spirit of Flagler, Mizner established his own factories to manufacture tile, ironwork, furniture, and pottery for his outstanding creations. Along with Mizner, thousands of businesses and individuals have benefited from the unfolding dream of Henry Morrison Flagler.

Exchange tragedy for improvement. Flagler was not only a man of great vision; he was also a man of victory. At the age of seventy-one he married thirty-four-year-old Mary Lily Kenan, his third wife, and continued to expand his vision of Palm Beach. When a fire destroyed the Palm Beach Inn in 1903, Flagler, who was seventy-three at the time, rebuilt it immediately in an even more lavish style and renamed it The Breakers.

Leave a legacy for the next generation. When the hotel burned to the ground a second time in 1925, it was Mary Lily's heirs who rebuilt The Breakers again, this time into a six-million-dollar majestic resort fashioned after the most outstanding Italian villas of the day. Some twelve hundred craftsmen and seventy-five artists from Italy completed the building in a record-breaking eleven and a half months. The twin belvedere towers and graceful arches of the exterior were inspired by Italy's famous Villa Medici, and the fountain in front of the hotel is patterned after the one in the Boboli Gardens of Florence. The heirs' ambition was to construct a fitting tribute to the vision and foresight of Henry Flagler, a goal they fully achieved.

Today Palm Beach continues as the home of millionaires and celebrities whose mansions mirror the unique grandeur of The Breakers. The late John Lennon had an oceanside residence there. Estee Lauder, of cosmetics fame, has resided in Palm Beach for many years. The famous Mar-A-Lago, former estate of breakfast-food heiress Marjorie Meriweather Post and now owned by Donald Trump, occupies seventeen acres and includes a nine-hole golf course. The Kennedy compound is world famous for a variety of reasons.

One romantic, scenic route through the city is its bicycle trail, covering 4.8 miles of magnificent scenery and architecture. And, of course, a visit to Palm Beach would not be complete without a stroll along Worth Avenue, one of the most exclusive shopping districts in the world. Here the leisurely, subtropical ambiance of Florida blends with the sophistication of Manhattan and the glitz of Beverly Hills. More than two hundred world-renowned specialty shops, posh department stores, gourmet restaurants and art galleries beckon to the tourist. Even a dog's life is a little better here: Worth Avenue features tiled drinking stations along the sidewalk for your canine's comfort.

Palm Beach continues its international legacy, proudly seated on the "Gold Coast" of the Atlantic Ocean. She is showy confirmation of man's ability to achieve excellence. And her palms whisper a quiet message: Whenever your "Old World" becomes cloudy and confining, remember the ingenuity of Henry Flagler. Then take heart! With some imagination and persistence, there's bound to be a "New World" somewhere, just waiting for you to discover and develop it.

8 FORT LAUDERDALE

Your Ship Is on Its Way!

Welcome to a city on the move! Whether you're looking for action or relaxation, Fort Lauderdale is the place. Three hundred miles of canals, lagoons, and rivers and countless miles of Atlantic beaches have caused this city to be called the "Venice of America."

Fort Lauderdale's waters are renowned for fishing, diving, swimming, and sunbathing. But they are best known for their boating. That's how the city earned another nickname: the Yachting Capital of the World.

There was a time, in the 1950s, when popular films caused Fort Lauderdale to be recognized as the place "where the boys are." Today the city caters to those who want to know where the *boats* are. It is the home port of more than eighteen thousand pleasure boats and virtually every luxury cruise line. It is *the* place to be if you are "waiting for your ship to come in."

Back in the 1800s, one of Florida's most popular pleasures was to linger at the docks, awaiting a ship from afar loaded with exotic wares and fascinating people. Because domestic goods were scarce and European imports were a luxury, Americans of all economic walks of life could be found "waiting for their ship to come in." Today, the phrase continues as a statement of hope for wealth or success.

You've probably seen the popular T-shirt: "When my ship came in, I was at the airport." Many men and women are still sitting at the dock, wishing and hoping for some exotic arrival from afar. Others are racing against time but traveling in circles. Sometimes we have to ask ourselves some very important questions.

- What are we waiting for?
- Why are we rushing around the same course we've been following for years, getting nowhere fast?
- What's our final destination?

Consider the infamous yacht, *Mercedes*. Years ago, it was caught in a storm and tossed about in a wildly shifting wind. Somehow the boat landed in socialite Mollie Wilmont's yard and was eventually sunk. It had started out all right, but without a sense of direction, it ended up going nowhere.

If there is to be a ship of opportunity in our future, we have to start now, paying careful attention at all times to the compass. Most of all, we need to have a definite destination in mind as well as a scheduled arrival time.

Here are a few more questions to help you chart your course:

- Am I really content to live the rest of my life the way things are right now?
- What do I want out of life?

- What is my purpose for living?
- What is expected of me?

Fort Lauderdale is a great example of a city that plotted out a destination for itself. In the early 1900s the city was anything but sparkling and glamorous. But someone had enough vision to refurbish it with an elaborate system of waterways. The sludge of the swamps was dredged and drained, and the ensuing metamorphosis changed the city from a loser into a winner.

That spirit of transformation might be what has drawn a host of modern-day successes into the area. Alamo Rental Car and Blockbuster Video are both based here. World-famous Dave Thomas of Wendy's has taken up residence in the city. And not to be forgotten is the incredible Swap Shop, a one-of-a-kind attraction extravaganza. Each of these successful ventures plotted its course, rode out the storms and winds, and carefully brought its ship in.

Swap Shop. Where can you go to shop, sample a variety of ethnic foods, get a haircut, watch first-run movies on eleven drive-in screens, play a variety of video games, ride a Ferris wheel, *and* see a million-dollar circus 365 days a year? Live elephants, horses, and daring high-wire acts are but a few of the offerings at Fort Lauderdale's singular Swap Shop, where admission is always *free*.

What began twenty-nine years ago as a ten-acre, six-vendor flea market has evolved into eighty acres of twenty-two hundred vendors, drawing more than thirteen million visitors a year. No expense has been spared to give you free admission and discount prices.

With this kind of success, you'd think that founder Preston Henn would coast, but the Swap Shop is in the midst of a ten-year plan, adding new buildings and more merriment.

Obviously, the dazzling entertainment, the thrill of the bargain hunt, and the immensity of the place attract millions of tourists. The star of the show, however, is the Swap Shop's unique money-back guarantee on its merchandise.

My favorite part of the Swap Shop is the opportunity it offers to virtually anyone of becoming an entrepreneur almost overnight. Take a walk around this cultural melting pot, listen to the variety of foreign languages dominating the conversations, and you see the American dream coming true every day. With two to three thousand dollars, a new American citizen can stock a shop and open a business without the hassle of a home office. Setup can be as simple as a few tables and a cashbox. And the public is delighted. "Swap till you drop," and there is still more to see and do. The Swap Shop may have found the success to retailing—happy vendors with low overhead and delighted shoppers who keep coming back for that one item they might have overlooked.

Wendy's. One of Fort Lauderdale's most famous residents is Dave Thomas. He can be seen most any day in a television commercial in the role of the slightly out-of-step, folksy Dave eating at one of his own Wendy's restaurants. He tells the world that Wendy's offers the best in service, quality, and taste. The chain's annual three billion dollars in sales provide ample evidence that somebody believes him!

Thomas's love for restaurants spans five decades, beginning with a dream at age eight and a restaurant job at the age of twelve. He joined the army at age eighteen and worked as a cook. But Dave didn't just cook. He improved the menu. Then he went to work on the appearance of the mess hall, brightening it up with paint. He did such a good job he was offered the assistant manager's spot in the enlisted men's club.

Afterward it seemed only natural to move into a civilian restaurant position. That's when he met his mentor, Colonel Harland Sanders of Kentucky Fried Chicken fame. Dave quickly realized that this was a man who had much to teach him. He signed on, earning $135 a week as a manager and receiving a rich legacy of insight and marketing savvy that ultimately led him to own his own KFC restaurant. Just six years later, Thomas sold his restaurant and became a thirty-five-year old millionaire. He went on to be a regional director of KFC until a lifelong ambition to own his own hamburger restaurant could wait no longer. In 1969 Dave realized his dream when he opened Wendy's Old-Fashioned Hamburgers in downtown Columbus, Ohio.

Success came quickly, but then it fled like a runaway train. Wendy's hit a disastrous slump in the 1980s. What was Dave to do? Simple. Try it again, and do it better. This time he hired a man named Jim Near to assist him, and together they turned the business operations around. It's been said, "The second time's a charm," but with Dave the charm was really success given birth by hard work and firm principles such as:

- Commitment to renewal and to superior standards. This is personally and consistently communicated to all franchisees.

- Reorganization of field operations. Hundreds of administrative positions were cut, and a few friends were lost along the way. Nonetheless, Thomas and Near felt this was imperative to strengthen the business.

- A "We Share" stock option. The program enabled employees to buy into the company. An entrepreneurial spirit was born in employees at all levels, who now felt an ownership in the company.

The story of Wendy's restaurants lends credence to Dave Thomas's belief:

Success is just as sweet
the second time around.

Alamo. Turn to the yellow pages for automobile rentals, and there's a good chance Alamo will be the first listing. Gimmick number one: Start the company name with an *A*. Of course that's not all it takes to beat out the big four competitors—Hertz, Avis, National, and Budget—so what's a latecomer like Alamo to do?

- Be the first to offer the money-saver of unlimited mileage at no extra charge (now mimicked by other rental companies in most cities).

- Become a price-cutter and advertise it in a big way. Alamo's prices are as much as 20 percent less than its major competitors.

- Initiate a program called "Best Friends" to retrain all four thousand employees in the art of friendly, courteous customer service.

- Keep costs down. Alamo's profit margins range between 3 and 5 percent—better than Hertz and second only to Avis. A great deal of research goes into selecting Alamo locales, and the stocking of cars is done according to traffic demand. Rental counters are a few miles down the road from the airport where rents are considerably lower. Customers are offered a short, complimentary van ride in exchange for substantial savings.

Today, Alamo reports revenues of more than five hundred million dollars a year, cornering an impressive percentage of the airport rental car market.

Blockbuster Video. Blockbuster chairman H. Wayne Huizenga is also owner of the NHL's Florida Panthers and baseball's Florida Marlins. Huizenga is versatile and innovative. He has carefully built the booming video business with an experienced, successful staff, and the profits just keep on rising.

Here are some of Blockbuster's navigating techniques:

- Set up a one-stop superstore so customers never feel the need to go anywhere else. Blockbuster stocks thousands of titles to suit an endless variety of tastes.

- Keep the family happy. Blockbuster stores carry no pornography or X-rated movies. A children's video section and a kids' video playhouse entertain the little ones while moms and dads browse uninterrupted. Blockbuster proudly announces itself as "America's Family Video Store."

- Focus on a base of profit-making inventory. Rentals ensure repeat business and high profits on a product that is completely paid for after approximately thirteen rentals. What doesn't rent is sold at giveaway prices.

• Inventory is reviewed often to keep customers happy. Thousands of favorite films and instructional tapes are chosen based on reviews and box-office success.

• National ad campaigns turn the huge industry into the consumer's friendly down-the-street store. "America's Most Important Videos Are Free" is a unique program offering public-service tapes on safety, parenting, and current issues without charge.

Blockbuster has made it tough on its competitors by renting one million videos nationwide a day, and their slogan "Wow! What a difference!" defines why.

Businesses in Fort Lauderdale aren't the only ones grasping opportunity; churches are too. Coral Ridge Presbyterian Church, pastored by Dr. D. James Kennedy, began with seventeen members who met each week in a cafeteria. It has grown to a present membership of more than eight thousand Christians who meet in a beautiful facility. Kennedy has launched an international ministry, teaching laypersons to better understand their personal faith. One by one, person to person, the endeavor has reached millions of people in more than one hundred countries.

First Baptist Church of Fort Lauderdale has just built a sanctuary of architectural wonder and beauty, one of the most beautiful I have seen anywhere in the world. This church understands that sometimes people need a little help finding their ship of dreams. Every Thanksgiving the church sets up a huge outdoor cafeteria for five thousand people called "The Feast of Plenty." Those who are homeless, indigent, or needing an extra helping hand are served a hot turkey dinner. They receive a gift of clothing, they see and hear an entertaining program, and they are offered good news of hope. I spoke there a few years ago, and it was one of the most moving events I have ever been a part of.

Each one of these Fort Lauderdale enterprises has a similar history. Figuratively, each began as a small boat and evolved into a massive cruise ship. Each has had storms to weather, repairs to make, and crew problems to contend with, but it has plotted the course, ridden out the wind and high seas, and come into the port. And when these ships came in, the owners were already on board, in full charge, and enjoying the sweetness of their success!

9 MIAMI

Keep the Dream Alive

Millions of Americans were first introduced to Miami through television's "Jackie Gleason Show." Then came "Miami Vice" and "The Golden Girls"—one depicting the glittery fast lane and the other offering a humorous look into retirement life. The city's fabled settings and scenery keep her in great demand as a backdrop for all sorts of film and photography shoots. You'll want to schedule some time for people watching in the variety of multicultural street scenes.

Miami's kaleidoscope of neighborhoods includes Little Cuba, the Haitian community, trendy Coconut Grove (a former hippy haven), elite Coral Gables, and other sprawling developments of every economic status. Perhaps Miami's most unique feature is her Art Deco section of 650 individual, pastel buildings in cotton-candy colors of peach, turquoise, lavender, mint, and peach. Stretched across the sky like a tropical rainbow, they are artistically graced with mermaids, waves, and flying porpoises.

Like a spicy bowl of gumbo, Miami's diverse ethnic groups manage to retain their distinct flavors. The multinational city is comprised of Cubans, Caribbean islanders, Seminole Indians, and retired northerners. "Snowbirds" come down from the North for the winter; "Snowflakes" jet in and out from their other homes. Just ninety miles off the coast of Cuba, Miami's shores beckon thousands of immigrants with the tempting call of freedom and an opportunity for a better life.

One a trip to the Keyes, my family and I found ourselves caught in one of Florida's frequent torrential cloudbursts as we passed through Miami. Since we needed fuel anyway, I pulled into a Miami gas station to wait out the storm. As Diane, the girls, and I talked, I noticed a little boy inside the cashier's cubicle. Obviously bored, he bounded outside the minute the downpour was over.

In Florida, the sun comes out quickly after a rain, and often only a few puddles remain after everything else dries within minutes. As I got out of the car to pump gas, I heard the little boy exclaim, "Daddy, Daddy, come quick! Look at all the dead rainbows lying on the ground!"

Dead rainbows? I had to see this for myself! Sure enough, there in the puddles I saw what the child meant. The mixture of oil, gas, water, and sunlight had produced swirls of colors. Of course! Dead rainbows! What else would you call them?

I just couldn't get that phrase out of my mind. *Dead rainbows.* It so aptly describes the dashed hopes of many men and women I meet who have given up and have begun mourning the death of their dreams. Perhaps it's due to the "instant" technology we've become accustomed to, but we seem to be giving up and giving in much too easily these days.

Driving through the streets, I saw the many immigrants and refugees eking out a new life through sheer willpower, and

I was reminded of the many stories of hardships endured on the road to hope and freedom.

More than half a million Cubans fled to Miami between 1959 and 1961 as Castro's revolution increased the oppression of the Cuban people. Another large exodus occurred in 1980 when about 125,000 sun-baked Cuban refugees arrived on Miami's shores, seeking a haven of comfort and solace.

Today they continue to stream in, not only from Cuba, but from Haiti. They endure tremendous hardships and face possible death just for the chance of carrying their dream of prosperity across the waters. For these people, Miami's Indian name of *Mayaime*, meaning "sweet water," is a literal reality. As one immigrant said, "Misery in another country is prosperity in Haiti."

Such courageous travelers aren't willing to wait around for someone else to resuscitate their rainbows or lift them into the sky. They know their only chance for hope, apart from a touch of divine grace, is within their own power. Like them, only you and I can decide how today will affect tomorrow and how we can turn difficult circumstances to our advantage.

In my travels around Miami, across the nation, and throughout the world through forty countries, I have discovered five basic types of individuals. Their hopes and dreams, or the lack of them, are always found in their conversations. Perhaps you know some of these people:

Wishers. This describes the majority of people. They go through life daydreaming, hoping, and longing.

They say, "If only I could . . . (get out of debt, buy a new car, be transferred to another city, have more friends)."

They sigh, "Someday . . . (things will be better, I'll go back to school, make more money, organize my life)."

If you happen to run into this kind of a dreamer six months later, he or she will still be talking about the same "if only" and "someday."

Wishers are lost in some indefinite time zone between today and tomorrow. Their conversations echo the words of comedian Lily Tomlin, who said, *I always wanted to be somebody, but I should have been more specific.*

Whiners stand alongside the wishers. For them, nothing is ever quite right, and life's troubles are always someone else's fault. They devote far more energy to defining the setback than to improving the situation. Like the Chinese proverb, they are *Noisy on outside—empty on inside.*

When given the choice between performance and excuses, whiners stick with the latter because it requires no sacrifice or responsibility.

Wanderers move from job to job, looking for an easy way to make "the big deal" happen. They also travel from friend to friend, hoping someone will consistently see things their way. Like pelicans waiting by the shrimp dock for scraps, they are too lazy to find their own source of fulfillment. Wanderers are easily led to alcohol and drugs to escape the realities of life— and the pressure to be successful.

The wounded often become close friends with the wanderers. Living in some past melancholy state, they are never quite able to move beyond yesterday's failures or betrayals. They believe their yesterdays control their future, and success eludes them because of their chronic attitude of victimization. They are their own worst enemy.

As long as past pain
is allowed to rule,
it will rule without mercy.

Winners. Ah, I can always spot the winners in the group. They are not the loudest; in fact they are often the least vocal. Instead of drawing attention to themselves, they work hard and treat everyone else with respect, regardless of their station in life. These are the exceptional ones who don't just wait. Instead they *make things happen.* Willing to sacrifice whatever it takes today to ensure success, diligence is a winner's most recognizable trait.

As the years come and go, I've noticed that some losers have become winners. And, sad to say, sometimes the opposite is true. But one thing is clear: *Attitude* is the quality that fuels change from within, and *attitude* permeates every fiber of our being, every day of our lives.

It was a significant day for me when I looked in the mirror and recognized a tenacious spirit within myself. With Miami's brave immigrants as my example, I knew I could no longer blame others for my situation, indulge in pity about my past, or depend on anyone else to assist me. I firmly planted a list of goals in my mind and resolved:

If it is to be,
it's up to me.

Woodrow Wilson said:

We grow great by dreams. All big men are dreamers. They see things in the soft haze of a spring day or in the red fire on a long winter's evening. Some of us let these great dreams die, but others nourish and protect them, nourish them through bad days until they bring them to the sunshine and light, which comes always to those who sincerely hope that their dreams will come true.

I firmly agree with Wilson! *Keep the dream alive! Never believe your rainbows are dead, but valiantly lift them to life, drawing strength from the vibrancy of their colors and the reality of their hope.*

10 ALLIGATOR ALLEY

A Little Help from Your Friends . . .

In a dual effort to make the Everglades more accessible to tourists and to cut a reasonable supply path to outlying cities, a fifty-mile stretch of desolate road was born many years ago. It was known by Floridians as "Alligator Alley." When my friends and I were teenagers, this highway was our path from Fort Myers to Miami and the rock concerts.

Noted on maps as Highway 84, Everglades Parkway, the road runs east and west from Naples to Fort Lauderdale, passing through the Big Cypress Seminole Indian Reservation, part of the Big Cypress National Preserve, and smack through the middle of the Everglades.

If you decide to take Highway 84 yourself, don't count on too much diversion along the way. Except for the Indian reservation, your only distractions will probably be wildlife. And if you decide to stop and explore, remember to stay on the boardwalks and out of the swamps. As anybody can tell you: The gators are real and they still think they own the place!

Capable of turning in seconds, an alligator can use its forceful tail to quickly (and literally!) disarm a person, and its toothy jaws can snap shut with three thousand pounds of pressure per square inch. If you happen to spot a gator sunning along the roadside, be sure to keep your distance. If you don't, you may find a new meaning for the term *snapshot.*

Above the highway, turkey vultures survey the land as they make broad sweeps across the sky, stopping at will to feast on roadside carrion. The water bordering the roadway is teeming with life, providing the fish-eating birds and alligators a natural, satisfying diet. Red-shouldered hawks peer down at the traffic, and in the early morning you might glimpse a graceful, white-tailed deer scampering along the roadside.

Tricolored herons wobble on spindly legs as they stalk their prey with needle-like beaks, and snowy egrets are a common sight. Nature abounds in all her glory, corrupted only by man's construction projects and ugly (but necessary) chain-link fences.

To this day, crossing Alligator Alley is an adventure to me. I still like to search out new wildlife. And I enjoy observing the fascinating habits of the various species as they attempt to co-exist with man's "improvements."

That is how I came to notice a small turtle perched atop a fence post one day. It seemed very happy, almost oblivious to anything except the sun and sleep, and very safe from slithering predators; still, I couldn't help but wonder how it got up there. The gift of safety had to have been bestowed upon it by a "friend," most certainly human.

As safe as the turtle was at that moment, however, if it was to continue to feed and survive, another friendly person would have to take it down. And if the little turtle could have spoken to me, it probably would have said, "Hey, none of us gets to the top in life without a little help from our friends."

On another occasion, I spotted a larger turtle, right in the middle of the road, moving as slowly as only a turtle can. Seeing absolute destruction in its immediate future, I donned my super-hero cape and went to its rescue. I gently reached down, careful not to frighten it. All at once, in a fit of ingratitude, the brown, reptilian creature shot out a six-inch neck and its massive set of teeth latched on to my hand.

This, I quickly discovered, was not just any turtle; it was a Florida snapping turtle. Again and again I tried to reach out to it, but the only response I got was a painful "snap." After several minutes, I could see no other recourse than to "kick its tail" right on over to the safety of the grass.

This turtle refused my help and wouldn't believe me when I tried to tell it of the impending danger. It didn't seem to understand that I could see the whole picture, and it could only see a few feet ahead. Driving away, nursing my sore hand, I asked myself, *Why are some people so afraid of the help of others? They would rather risk failure than take a friend's advice or accept a little help. Sometimes only a swift, friendly "kick" will help them out of their potentially dangerous situation.*

I thought about some of the wonderful "turtle-movers" who have made significant changes in my life. One in particular is Dr. H. Fred Williams.

At the vulnerable age of nineteen, drug-free for only a year, newly married by just a few months, and hair down to my shoulders, I felt called into the ministry. Having no church background at all, I didn't know where to start, so I began a search for information.

I located a Stetson University extension course offering a course called Old Testament Survey. Once I signed up and began the classes, I quickly recognized that I was a "turtle"— slower and at a disadvantage to more experienced students. I was in desperate need of a lift up the pole of life.

You may have forgotten that I graduated from high school with honors—"Yes, your honor. No, your honor"—and a D average. I'm quite convinced that the school administrators decided to pass me for only one reason: They knew they'd never see me again if they did.

In any case, I can vividly remember the shock on the professor's face when he saw me. I'm sure he thought I wouldn't last the term. But I kept coming back, and each night I waited around after class to ask him questions. No one told me I was an unlikely candidate to lead a congregation, least of all my teacher, "Dr. Fred."

Naive as I was, I invited Fred Williams to our home one night after class. That visit began a long, mentoring relationship that continued every Monday night in our humble apartment for the next year—and for many years after we had moved on.

It was Dr. Williams who gave me my first professional opportunity. It was he who conducted my ordination. Eventually I did cut my hair, but he never said a word about it. In true wisdom, Fred Williams concentrated on helping me grow from the inside out.

Before long, I was pastoring my first little church in Immokalee, Florida, and living on seventy-five dollars a week. The stories I could tell you about my first funeral and wedding would put you in stitches. But there were some other turtle-movers there too. Kindhearted people like the Carraways and the Tillmans covered my tracks when necessary and gently advised me. And somehow, just when we needed help the most, a few extra dollars or groceries would appear.

A year later, we left for Charleston, South Carolina, and a full-time education. There, the Eckenrodes, relatives I had never met, helped Diane find a job and let us live with them until we could get on our feet. Once again, I was being helped across the road, and this time I graduated cum laude.

My intention is not to bore you with meaningless details, but to give you a glimpse into the importance of "turtle-helpers," no matter how small the lift may seem. Many, many wonderful relationships have come my way in life. And from them I have learned firsthand:

Successful people
enjoy helping others
become successful.

11 KEY LARGO

Somebody Still Loves You . . .

Key Largo, Montego, ooh, I wanna take you down to Kokomo. We'll get there fast and then we'll take it slow . . ." OK, so I can't sing. But the Beach Boys do have a point. There's nothing like a trip to Key Largo to give you that "laid-back" feeling.

In 1952 Humphrey Bogart and Lauren Bacall acted out an enchanting romance against the island's tranquil scenery. Ever since, tourists have cruised on down US 1 to experience the tiny key's charms. Its primary attraction is the John Pennekamp Coral Reef State Park, an underwater wonderland of fish and a panoramic sight of vibrant corals visible to the scuba diver and the snorkeler, or by glass-bottom boat.

When I first received the news of my daughter Melissa's worsening scoliosis and the inevitability of surgery, this seemed like the perfect place to get away while I thought through her immediate future. I headed down, hopeful that the buoyancy of the water would somehow lift my spirits.

As I donned my scuba gear it occurred to me that I probably wouldn't need my weight belt—the heaviness of my heart seemed sufficient to keep me down. I remember swimming with determined power kicks, trying to physically force the pain from my mind. I didn't want my little girl to hurt, and I prayed for peace. Down, down to the bottom of the sea I dove, looking for relief.

Suddenly there it was, waiting for me with open arms. I almost rammed right into it headfirst—the underwater statue of the Christ. At that moment, it became more than a statue to me. It was an instant reinforcement of the promise, *"Come unto me, and I will give you rest."*

All of a sudden, I found myself laughing. As I watched the behavior of my underwater companions, I soon realized they were mimicking the types of pressures in life. Read on . . .

Little pressures. Like the tiny minnows, these problems nibble away at our patience a little bit at a time. These are the difficult people, hurt feelings, strained relationships, a flat tire, a missed promotion, the mile-long "to do" list, an accidentally bounced check, the everyday errands and routines, deadlines— these are the minnows of life.

Serious pressures. Lurking in the background the moray eels want a real bite; they aren't interested in nibbles. Serious pressures are like that. I'm talking about the pink slip in an envelope, the doctor's report, a policeman at the door, a divorce or broken relationship, the unraveling of a much-needed business deal, betrayal by a friend, a child's need for surgery . . .

Unnamed pressures. At Pennekamp so many varieties of fish swim by so rapidly there is no time to attach a particular name or species to each one. These are the endless lists of decisions waiting for an answer, the traffic annoyances, blistering-hot days, phone calls as you're going out the door—distractions at every turn.

I watched as the minnows came and went at a frenetic pace, as the eel ventured in and out of its hole, as the fish continued to parade by. Still the statue remained, arms open wide, offering peace, confidence, and hope. Thirty feet under the water, with a regulator in my mouth, I began to sing, "Jesus loves me, this I know, for the Bible tells me so."

I swam to the surface, dropping my weights as a symbol of leaving my heavy heart behind. The pressure before me was indeed a serious one, but under the sea I had found a reminder of the sure promise of refuge and comfort in God's love. I left the reef, confident of the rest my spirit sought after and yearned for, ready to make the best decision for my daughter's future.

There aren't many things in this life that I can call absolutes, but this statement is unconditional in my belief:

> **There is nothing you can do**
> **to make God stop loving you;**
> **there is nothing you can accomplish**
> **To make Him love you more.**

After seminars or speeches I sometimes encounter individuals who confide in me that they are at the lowest point of their life.

Think about this: the lowest point on the earth is actually 6.8 miles deep in the Mariana Trench under the Pacific ocean. If you jumped into it carrying a one-pound steel ball, it would take you sixty-four minutes to fall all the way to the bottom. Even at that, when you finally arrived, God's love for you would already be there! The deepest well ever dug was an eight-mile-deep shaft in Russia; even this is not too deep for God's love to reach.

You and God—that is one relationship that time, circumstances, and even your enemies cannot destroy. Inflation, depression, economic fallout, government regulations, personal betrayal or attack, criticism, illness—none of these can rob you of His love. I have a bold, calculated certainty of this truth based on a sure promise: *"Be strong and of good courage: do not be afraid, nor be dismayed, for the LORD your God is with you wherever you go"* (Josh. 1:9).

Oprah Winfrey, in her nationally syndicated programs, has been closing her recent interviews with this question: "What do you know for certain?"

I would have to say, "Look, Oprah, I know this for certain: Jesus loves me, this I know. And no matter how far down you go, there is always Someone waiting who loves you."

12 ISLAMORADA

Putting the Past Behind

*I*slamorada—the name rolls off the tongue with gentle rhythm. One of thirty-two islands making up the Florida Keys, Islamorada nestles on a narrow strip of land in the midst of the vast Atlantic Ocean. The journey there, down US 1 from Miami, seems like a connect-the-dots adventure. You'll find yourself wondering if there isn't more bridge than land.

Go deep-sea fishing, scuba dive, enjoy dolphin entertainment at the Theatre of the Sea, or do nothing at all—that's part of the appeal of the small speck of land swimming in the Atlantic.

My memories of Islamorada are crowned by one particular trip there, taken so I could spend some quality time with my dad. It was our effort to play catch-up after all the years we'd spent apart while I was growing up. On that occasion, as I left his home and returned to my hotel, a spirit of restlessness overwhelmed my mind and body. Instead of going to bed, I found myself wandering outside to sit by the water as I watched the hotel's anchored boat bob up and down with the tide. *That's me!* I thought, *bouncing up and down from feeling good to feeling bad. I've got to get this thing worked out between Dad and me.*

Sitting by the water brought back countless childhood memories. I saw myself playing in the sand, swimming in the waves, and listening over and over to "Sitting on the dock of the bay . . ." The thought of those happy times brought a smile to my face.

As quickly as the good memories came, however, unhappy ones pushed them aside. I studied the gentle tide as it rippled across the wide expanse of ocean before me, hoping for a distraction. In the stillness of the night, the moon's reflection bounced off the water as though the moon and sea were playing catch with each other. I stared without seeing, recalling the recent events of the evening as well as those of the long-ago past.

Dad and I had talked for hours, but we'd said little. Nothing had been settled—nothing at all.

There was so much emotion pent up inside me, I wanted to scream. There were questions I wanted answered. There were years of bitterness and anger. They weighed against my heart like the anchor holding the hotel boat at the dock. Just as that buoyant boat longed to dance across the waves untethered, so my heart wanted to understand, to forgive.

How I wished we had really talked!

Just as I convinced myself that the opportunity was past, at least on this occasion, I was suddenly aware of another's presence. I looked up to find my six-foot-two dad towering over me.

"Can we talk awhile, son?"

The words I'd longed to hear were finally spoken.

At first the conversation picked up where it left off—Dad was asking about my "doings" and I was trying to impress him with my success. But in the back of my mind was a lingering childhood impression of myself: *You're dumb; you'll never be anything.* It wasn't always communicated verbally, of course. Sometimes it was said in actions or in a lack of them. Nonetheless, the result was always the same.

I didn't measure up. I just wasn't good enough. In my adult life I had been desperately trying to prove it wasn't true.

Something changed that night. As I looked at Dad, I could feel the root of bitterness beginning to loosen its stranglehold inside me. I began to see him with eyes of compassion. I wondered if maybe he, too, hadn't been the victim of a hopeless past.

What had hurt me the most had been the overwhelming sense of abandonment I'd felt when Dad left us. He had left when I was only six. A few years later I had become the victim of both sexual and physical abuse. I'd written letter after letter, begging him to come and get me, but he'd never answered. Meanwhile, my mother had moved us from place to place, trying to make it financially. We had been terribly poor.

I studied his face, wondering *How could you not have cared about your own son?*

Questions poured out of me as though a retaining wall had suddenly given way. I wanted to know about his leaving. His apparent lack of concern. The letters he never wrote.

Dad looked at me—I mean for the first time I can remember, he *really* looked at me. I saw the pain on his face. "Jay, I never got any of these letters. I never knew . . ."

Maybe Mom had never mailed the letters. Maybe Dad, who was always moving himself, had never received them. I'll never know.

I learned quite a few lessons that night—for example, that there are three sides to every story: your side, the other side, and the true side. But most of all, I had to view my father through eyes of compassion. I realized that this man had never intended to destroy me; he had been on his own trip of self-destruction. And the words he said to me that night were the best gift he could have offered: *"Jay, I know I wasn't much of a father. You've done incredibly well on your own and I am proud. Even though I wasn't there for you then, I want you to know that I am here for you now."*

As the tide washed in and out, delicately moving the sand and forming new designs, I felt a great sense of peace bathing my soul. An unexpected lifting of the heavy bitterness revealed a new heart in me. At last I understood. It wasn't anything I'd done wrong. It wasn't that Dad hadn't loved me, either. He had simply drowned in his own problems and alcohol addiction.

Before me was a decision. I could forgive, move forward, and begin building a new relationship of trust, caring, and friendship. Or I could continue allowing everything to be directed and colored by past feelings of inadequacy and anger.

I chose to move toward a fresh start by initiating a friendship with Dad. I couldn't begin with a father-son relationship right then. But as the friendship developed, so did the bonds of family we had never before experienced. Little by little, year by year, we are working to build new memories.

Today I can tell you about my dad with pride. His name is Jim Strack, a man who successfully dealt with his past and for the past thirty years has both personally and professionally dedicated his life to helping others break their own chains of addiction. He has taught me that a real man is man enough to say "I'm sorry" and to allow the mistakes of the past to improve the future.

Everyone has past pain. And to "shake off the dust" of the past requires us to A-C-T out a plan. Here are the decisions I made:

> **A**—Admit that anger and bitterness are controlling you, coloring your picture of life, and inflicting more pain.
>
> **C**—Choose to forgive the offenses. This choice is solely in your power and must be a conscious act of your will.
>
> **T**—Toss away your tendency to obsessively dwell upon the offensive memories. You cannot deny them, but you can decide to minimize their power over your mind.

I carry in my mind a vivid picture of putting away the hurt and dirt of the past. It comes from a Hebrew ceremony I once read about in my theology studies. In a solemn ritual, the priest would lay hands on the *scapegoat*. In so doing he laid the sins of the people upon the animal. The scapegoat was then sent away into the wilderness, bearing the sins of the people, never to be seen again. This is the ultimate picture for us

Total forgiveness is choosing to send away destructive, past memories and beginning life again, fresh and new.

The bottom line: You can hold on to the darkness and the pain if you want to. But their strongest influence will be over you, not over the one with whom you're angry. Whether it's an ex-spouse, a business partner, a friend, parent, or child, it doesn't really matter who's right or wrong. What counts is whether you are willing to make the best of a bad situation and freely move on.

In Islamorada, the view of the sunset dipping into the Gulf of Mexico is a spectacular one. And if you cross over to the other side of the narrow island, the majestic rising of the sun from the Atlantic Ocean is a wondrous sight too.

Symbolically, these actions remind me of "crossing over" to the other side of life: allowing the scars of former days to sink out of sight, looking toward the rising of a new set of hopes and dreams.

The past will always live on in memories. But it is within our power to override its tyranny with the power of forgiveness and with a strong, resolute belief in the future.

13 KEY WEST

Dances with Dolphins

Key West is more than an island on the south-ernmost tip of the United States. It is also a state of mind. When you get to Key West throw away your watch; here, time is measured in sunsets and sunrises.

Upon arrival, the visitor is immediately mesmerized by the uniqueness of the island. At every turn, there seems to be a "come-as-you-are" party under way. Where else do people celebrate the glory of a sunset with bagpipes, drums, and hurrahs? Even the old cemetery is shrouded in frivolity with hilarious epitaphs such as, "I told you I was sick," and "At least I know where he's sleeping tonight."

Getting to Key West is an adventure in itself. To do so,

you'll traverse one of the longest causeways in the world, yawning and stretching more than 150 miles across the Atlantic and connecting a tropical paradise of forty-five small islands. The engineering feat of constructing and combining forty-two bridges, including the Seven-Mile Bridge, is amazing. And the three-hour drive through Old Florida is an escapade all its own.

Artists and writers have found a haven of inspiration in Key West over the years. Hemingway lived here when he wrote *For Whom the Bell Tolls* and *A Farewell to Arms*. Harry Truman kept a presidential retreat in Key West, referred to as the Little White House. Visited there by dignitaries and celebrities alike, Truman made many history-shaping decisions in Key West, "where the clear air and blue skies made answers appear clearer." Both of these homes are open to the public and well worth strolling through.

Key West balances delicately in the midst of nowhere, as though the ocean has delivered her up in our honor. The Key West Aquarium includes a "touch tank" where visitors can personally meet the denizens of the deep. Longtime residents are referred to as "conchs," and all of the environment pays tribute to the sparkling waters.

Ah, the waters! Calming and invigorating at the same time, they hold in their depths millenniums of mystery. As a teenager, I spent many a summer on commercial fishing boats, some of which were anchored off Key West. And I was always captivated by the graceful glide of the dolphins through the water. For hours I watched, hoping for the sight of a glistening gray fin streaking through the sea.

Schools of twenty or thirty dolphins would challenge our boat in a race or frolic alongside. Since I was the only teenager aboard ship at the time, I imagined that these friendly creatures were my soul mates on an otherwise lonely journey.

I've since discovered that my vivid imaginings in those days were not so silly after all.

The *delphinus delphis*, as it is known scientifically, has been an inspiration throughout history, known for its tenacity, charm, intuitiveness, and intelligence. Dolphins have been called "man's best friend in the sea," and their strategies offer us incredible wisdom and insight for navigating in life's treacherous waters. Consider some of their habits:

They build strong family ties. It is believed dolphins maintain strong family relationships for as many as three generations. Dr. Randall Wells of the University of California at Santa Cruz has observed grandparents, parents, and baby dolphins traveling and playing together.

My family and I cherish the memory of watching a mother dolphin and her baby. Dive after dive, they danced in a synchronized ballet together. Intimacy among loved ones has a special potency all its own. The family unit, whether human or otherwise, was ordained from the beginning as the ultimate organization for providing affection, protection, and imitation.

Dolphins recognize the benefits of the sense of touch. Their skin is smooth as an inner tube and very sensitive. Members of the family groups often touch and rub against each other as a gesture of intimate, supportive encouragement.

They protect each other from sharks. Dolphin behavior around sharks is legendary. Members of a school protect their young when sharks attempt to kill and destroy them. As the shark approaches, the bigger dolphins attack it from both sides, using their hard snouts as weapons.

Sharks, on the other hand, believe in "looking out for number one." They travel alone; they hunt alone. Only one mammal has survived and succeeded in shark-infested waters: the dolphin.

The nineties have often been defined as a "shark-eat-shark" world. In marine life, there are 360 different types of sharks, but it is obvious that not all sharks are in the water. (More about that in a later chapter!)

They care for the weak and wounded. If a member of the dolphin group is hurt and sick, it sends out cries of distress, and soon help is on the way. The book *Dolphins: Our Friends in the Sea* by the National Geographic Society describes the fascinating account of a group of dolphins swimming up under an injured mammal to carry it to the surface for a breath.

Often I am called upon to intervene in a parent-teen relationship or a marriage in trouble. Too many times I find the damage is the result of overlooked hurt feelings or emotional pain. We must commit ourselves to assisting our loved ones at their point of need.

Dolphins learn to listen. One of the most unique features of dolphins is their hearing system, called "echo-location," which allows them to navigate by using sound waves. This helps them communicate, maneuver, and locate food in the ocean. To echo-locate, dolphins send out high-pitched clicking sounds, as many as twelve hundred per second, and seven to eight times higher in frequency than humans can hear. As the dolphin swims through the water, it scans for objects ahead through the sound-bouncing echo. Much like a computer, the dolphin's brain analyzes the echo and reports the location, size, and shape of an object.

Perhaps this reminds us that we should never pretend to know what we don't and that we should not feel ashamed to ask and learn. I once heard a Sunday school teacher say,

> *God gave you two ears*
> *and one mouth*
> *so that you can listen*
> *twice as much as you speak.*

A recent study in the *Journal of Business Communication* disclosed that good listeners hold higher-level positions. Lee Iacocca, former CEO of Chrysler Corporation, once said,

> *Listening can make the difference*
> *between a mediocre company*
> *and a great one.*

They cultivate a win-win lifestyle. Dolphins like to win, but they want others to win too. Several years ago, our family took its first swim with dolphins while exploring the Keys. It was a unique and awesome experience. Out of the three dolphins in the roped-off area, one in particular took an interest in my younger daughter, Christa. He used his snout to push her feet and mimicked her somersaults and spins in the water.

After a while, Christa grew tired of treading water and began to lag behind in the game. Swimming the short distance into the dock, she was suddenly surprised by a helping lift from behind. It was her dolphin buddy, helping her up onto the dock! As she sat catching her breath, the dolphin waited nearby for her to resume play.

I had to see it to believe it.

Stephen Covey, author of the best-selling *Seven Habits of Highly Effective People,* has defined the win-win paradigm by saying, "there is plenty for everybody, so that one person's success is not achieved at the expense or exclusion of the success of others." Everyone works together and takes into account what is mutually beneficial. In too many homes, organizations, and businesses, cooperation has been replaced with competition.

Dolphins are flexible. Of all the beneficial lessons we can learn from the dolphin, perhaps the one I value the most is the ability to "go with the flow." Dolphins' creative and quick thinking allows them to deal immediately with the situation at hand. If necessary, they can alter their behavior at a moment's notice.

Often we persist in an impossible situation or relationship because we are afraid of the unknown currents of change. Rudyard Kipling exposes the excuse of fear as a great deceiver:

Of all the liars of the world,
sometimes the worst are your own fears.

In the rapidly changing, innovative world of the 1990s, one key word will be *adapt.* Nothing is more permanent than change, and nothing is greeted with more resistance. The dance of the dolphin is a valuable metaphor for us as we navigate the deep and sometimes dangerous waters of life.

14 THE EVERGLADES

Leadership Secrets of the Eagle

Alligators. Water moccasins. Panthers. Indians. The Everglades swamp! For a ten-year-old boy, this sounded like the kind of adventure only TV could deliver! The thought of airboating through the Everglades was more exciting to me than words could communicate. Now a grown-up kid, I'm still fascinating by the Everglades, especially since I have since learned in geography classes that Florida's world-famous swamp is actually a river of grass that encompasses approximately one-fourth of the state.

This is Indian country, where the Seminole tribe now shares with nature the glades that once were home to the Calusa and Tequesta Indians. The original Indian name *Pa-hay-okee* (grassy waters) was changed to Everglades because it was believed that the river traveled through the glades like an eternal snake. In truth, the river's flow only touches a small part of the 1.5-million-acre Everglades National Park.

The Everglades' unique ecosystem includes some three hundred species of birds, six hundred kinds of fish, twenty-five types of mammals, and forty-five varieties of plant forms, all indigenous to the delicate environment. Although I'm now well beyond ten years old, I remember my boyhood visits here as though they were yesterday. I would sit in a boat for hours, watching the captivating parade of wildlife go by, each species seeming more unique than the last.

And then there's my absolute favorite Everglades pastime: eagle watching. This species truly is unforgettable.

Once you've seen an eagle in flight you immediately understand why it is called "the monarch of the sky." Its unique wing structure allows it to reign supreme in the heavens. No living creature, save man, can conquer it.

Proudly displayed throughout American history, the majesty and grandeur of the eagle have inspired humankind from cave dwellers to Belshazzar of Babylon, from Caesar to Charlemagne, from Napoleon to modern-day CEOs. In virtually every art form, eagles remain a favorite symbol of strength and honor.

Contemporary men and women in leadership could learn much from the Everglades' mighty eagles. Like the eagle, quality leaders have become something of an endangered species as an excess of fallen heroes has left us with a crisis of confidence. In the Everglades, the secrets of the eagle's edge on leadership can be observed in its distinctive, instinctive traits:

Stamina. While most of nature scurries for cover, eagles revel in the power of storms. They turn the wind's turbulence to their advantage, using it to fly higher, faster, and longer. Wind currents buoy eagles upward, conserving much of their own energy.

Quality leaders recognize that storms are inevitable. They look for ways to adapt the storms' energy into successful strategies. Instead of asking "Why is this happening to me?" a strong leader asks "What kind of an opportunity does this problem provide?" He or she uses mental toughness to transform stress into strength.

Solitude. Geese fly in gaggles and ducks fly in flocks, but eagles soar alone. We can choose to go through life honking and quacking or we can mount up on eagles' wings. Even if you work with a bunch of "turkeys," you can decide to soar through the heavens!

A leader is willing to go it alone when he or she believes what he or she is doing is right. The risk of going against the flow, the popular, or the expected is a challenge we've faced since childhood. And this is the type of decision that ultimately builds character.

We ought to ask ourselves the simple question:

> *Who am I*
> *when no one else is looking?*

Viewpoint. The eagle selects its perspective carefully. Perched higher than any other living creature, its powerful vision scopes out the environment for miles around. It is capable of discerning a rabbit two miles away, and it can swoop down and dive at its prey at up to two hundred miles an hour with precision. Once the eagle selects a target it moves quickly, and escape is almost always hopeless.

Strong leaders also study "the big picture." Taking time to gather all available information, they are ready when the time comes to execute decisions quickly and accurately. Once they decide to advance forward, they do so without a thought of turning back.

Home life. Perhaps the secret to the majesty and supremacy of the eagle has to do with the significance it places on home life:

• Eagles mate for life. An airboat guide in the Everglades once told me of a pair of eagles whose nest had been in the same spot for over twenty-three years. The nest needed repairs, but the majestic couple never gave up on each other.

- Eagles take great care in building their nests. Animal fur and bird feathers are used to make the nests pillow soft. We all know, deep inside, that *the way things go in the nest will determine the rest.* I have written in my journal,

> *You are only the leader*
> *you are at home.*

- *Eagles enable their young to be independent.* When the time comes to leave home, the parent eagles begin, little by little, to remove the softness from the nest. Eventually the uncomfortable, uncushioned thistles and sticks force the young to leave and soar independently. The mother or father eagle drop the young out of the nest, then bear them up on their own wings. They do this over and over—the goal is to enable the younger, weaker birds to gain strength and to soar on their own. The parent doesn't give up until the goal is achieved.

Everyone (even an eagle) needs a push now and then!

We face incredible odds in our attempt to lead in the home, on the job, and in society. The importance of "family first" is often minimized by public, peers, and politics. And many times, efficiency as a manager is chosen over effectiveness as a leader. When it comes to family, our most cherished possession, the "one-minute manager" just won't do the job.

Learning from the eagle means we develop a sense of leadership. And strong leadership requires much of everyone, both of those who lead and of those who follow. As a zealous soldier once proclaimed,

> *Lead,*
> *go behind,*
> *or get out of the way!*

15 NAPLES

Golf Lessons for the Game of Life

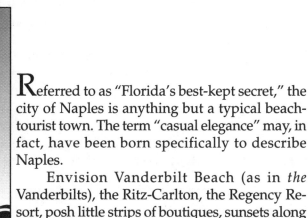

Referred to as "Florida's best-kept secret," the city of Naples is anything but a typical beach-tourist town. The term "casual elegance" may, in fact, have been born specifically to describe Naples.

Envision Vanderbilt Beach (as in *the* Vanderbilts), the Ritz-Carlton, the Regency Resort, posh little strips of boutiques, sunsets along the beach, Rolls-Royces as common as palm trees, million-dollar homes, and lots and lots of golf-course communities. You have just imagined the city of Naples, Florida.

This is one of my favorite golfing areas because of the variety and number of courses. You can play every day for a month and never visit the same course twice. There are reportedly more fairways per capita in Naples than anywhere else in the world. And to add to your temptation, perfect golf weather awaits you almost any day of the year.

And if inexperience or poor skill is holding you back, give the David Ledbetter Golf Academy a call. Located at the prestigious country-club community of Quail West in North Naples, the academy is founded and operated by David Ledbetter, the famous swing doctor and adviser to the pros. If you're near Orlando, you can "swing by." Ledbetter's original golf school at the incredibly beautiful Lake Nona Golf and Country Club, recently ranked thirty-seventh in the country.

With more than one thousand golf courses, Florida has an edge of almost two hundred over the runner-up state. That ratio continues as Florida plans and constructs more courses. Visiting Florida without playing golf is like traveling through Italy without eating pasta. You can do it, but the temptation is everywhere!

As *The Florida Survival Handbook* says, "Golf and Florida. The first is a state of mind; the second a state full of golf courses." Even if you play really poorly, Florida's golf courses deserve a visit, if just for the fabulous scenery!

Growing up on "the wrong side of the tracks," I didn't have the chance to play golf until college. These days, I love the game, but I only play sporadically because of my speaking schedule. I am, however, a devoted hacker. (As I write this, my ball retriever is at the pro shop being regripped.) Actually, golf is a very broadening sport—I ended up learning to scuba dive in order to recover my lost golf balls!

One reason I find golf so intriguing is that I learn a great deal about the person I am playing with, as well as about myself. Here are a few golf lessons that double as lessons in the game of life:

Pay attention to basics. Too many golfers attempt to polish their technique before mastering the basics of grip, stance, and aim. A bad grip can't produce a good swing, and a lazy aim will never hone in on the target.

Along the same lines,

> *Put more effort into the basics of life:*
> *integrity, humility, fidelity, courage,*
> *and the Golden Rule.*

Small things count big. A five-foot putt can give you the win as surely as a 250-yard drive. Sinking putts builds confidence: *I did it! I can do it again!* Don't put all your confidence in the long shot; ultimately, it's the guy who can get the ball in the hole who wins the game.

And in life the same concepts hold true: Don't underestimate the validity of the small accomplishment; it can be the final step toward the big one. The person who accomplishes small goals moves on to grander schemes. Or as an ancient teaching points out,

> *He who is faithful over little*
> *will be given the opportunity*
> *to be faithful over much.*

Use positive self-talk. Sports psychologist Dr. Richard Coop challenges golfers: "If we were caddying for ourselves and talked to ourselves as negatively as we do during most rounds, we would end up firing ourselves."

Coop says a good caddie is positive and supportive of his player, providing encouragement after every play. Caddies are analytical of the play rather than of the person, speaking constructively about how to improve the situation.

As you confront the challenges of daily living, believe in yourself; tell yourself *I can do it.* Attack the plan, not yourself. Complement yourself when you achieve; encourage yourself when you fail. Look at it this way—if you don't, who will?

Most mistakes are made before the swing. The swing is the result of preparation. If your grip, stance, or aim is off, your swing will be inferior. Give your mind over to getting ready, *then* swing. And remember the words of Roy Black, renowned defense attorney:

The will to win doesn't mean anything
because everyone wants to win.
It is the will to PREPARE to win
that makes the difference.

Focus on the task at hand. Shut out the rest of the world and aim your shot right on target. Center your thoughts on where you want the ball to go regardless of spectators or other distractions. Stay focused on the goal. In particular, don't measure success by the score of the other players. You've got to play *your* game regardless of how they do.

As Henry Ford once said,

Whether you think you can
or think you can't,
you are right.

Put mind over muscle. Disorganized thinking can flush hours of practice and years of playing down the drain. The accomplished golfer directs the body to do exactly what the mind is thinking.

It is within your own power to control your time and will. *Success requires a commitment from the mind, the spirit, and the body.*

One correction can save five strokes. If you have a bad slice, it stays with you through every hole. Correct it once and for all, and you improve your score dramatically.

Whether you're a golfer or not, go ahead and kill a bad habit as soon as you become aware of it.

Thomas Harris is quoted as saying,

Blaming your faults
on your nature
does not change the nature
of your faults.

Concentrate on the swing, not on the ball. The ball isn't the goal; the pin is. My good friend Zig Ziglar reminds me,

"Who you become and what you learn on the way to the goal are more important than the goal itself."

Visualize the shot. Famous teacher to the pros Harvey Penick once sent a telegram to a player in a championship playoff with three words of advice:

Take dead aim!

Penick urges the golfer to keep this thought all the way through the course. Put your concentration into the yardage ahead, clearly focusing on what it takes to send the drive down the fairway. See the spot on the green, shut out all else, and visualize the ball going right where you send it.

Take this principle home with you, to the office, and into the world. *Keep a mental picture of the accomplished, successful goal in your mind.*

Put a bad shot behind you. Instead of reliving what went wrong, step up to the next shot with all confidence. Concentrate on what you know is the right way to do it and give it 100 percent. Agonizing over the last mistake may produce another. Thomas J. Watson has said,

Success lies on the far side of failure.

Don't look at obstacles. One LPGA caddie told me she doesn't look at the obstacles. Her only concern is, "How do we get it down the fairway to the hole?" Once that path is determined, all energy of the mind and body works toward it.

Our natural inclination is to give a great amount of energy to overcoming obstacles. But the wiser alternative is to concentrate on the path to the goal.

Keep calm in "sudden death." When it's down to just you and one other player, keep the self-talk going. Don't give the win away now, just because you're nervous. Instead, utilize the anxiety as extra energy. Sudden death or not, your preshot routine and your concentration have to be the same as on every other shot; this is just another hole.

Remember, you are good enough to have come this far. Follow through with all you've got. Even if you don't win, you'll finish looking good!

Public Golf Courses in Florida You Don't Want to Miss

Coral Oaks Golf Course, Cape Coral. Designed by Arthur Hill, the course is rated among the top fifty municipal courses in the United States. Yardage: 6,623. Par: 72. Slope: 123.

Eastwood Golf Course, Fort Myers. Listed by *Golf Digest* as one of the top fifty public courses for ten years in a row. Designed by Robert von Hagge and Bruce Devlin. Yardage: 6,772. Par: 72. Slope: 130.

Emerald Dunes, West Palm Beach. Designed by Tom Fazio and voted by golf course architects as the best-designed public course to open during 1987–1991. Yardage: 6,775. Par: 72. Slope: 132.

Golden Ocala Golf Course, Ocala. If you've ever wanted to play the world-famous holes, come here to experience the replicas of eight of them. Designed by Ron Garl and architect Bob Spence, it ranks in *Golf Digest*'s top seventy-five public courses. Yardage: 6,775. Par: 72. Slope: 132.

Hunters Creek Golf Course, Orlando. Four sets of tees are offered to compensate for the tremendous distances of this long course. Lloyd Clifton designed Hunters Creek, considered one of the country's best public courses. Yardage: 7,432. Par: 72. Slope: 127.

Lely Flamingo, Marco Island. This is a Robert Trent Jones Sr. course with an island hole on the fourteenth. Yardage: 7,171. Par: 72. Slope: 135.

The Links at Key Biscayne, Key Biscayne. Ranked among the nation's top thirty public courses by *Golf Digest* and designed by Robert von Hagge and Bruce Devlin. Its signature seventh hole is a 434-yarder, rated among the toughest in Florida. Yardage: 7,070. Par: 72. Slope: 138.

Pelican's Nest, Bonita Springs. Here you can see native Florida in all its glory as you walk through a landscape of palmetto, pines, mangroves, natural vegetation, and lakes. Tom Fazio designed the original eighteen holes, and another nine holes have been added. Yardage: 6,950. Par: 72. Slope: 138.

West Palm Beach Country Club, West Palm Beach. Opened in 1947, the course encompasses two hundred acres interwoven with Australian pines and other native trees. It is the first course designed entirely by Dick Wilson and is set on rolling land, something you won't see much of in Florida. Yardage: 6,789. Par: 72. Slope: 124.

One final word—many challenging and fabulous resort courses are open to you throughout Florida if you choose to vacation on their properties. The Walt Disney courses and the Hyatt's Grand Cypress course, all in the Orlando area, are just a few of the examples.

16 FORT MYERS

Keep At It!

"Oh no, not the Edison Home! Not today!"

I'd heard all about this place from classmates who'd already been here.

"No touching. No talking. Single file."

At eleven, as the mischievous class clown, I could think of nothing worse than being trapped in some scientist's tiresome old house. Like it or not, however, our field trip was inevitable.

I walked into the winter home and laboratory of Thomas Alva Edison with a bad attitude, expecting to experience boredom upon boredom. But it didn't take long for fascination to replace frustration. I was unexpectedly enthralled by what I discovered.

First, the lushness of the gardens made me feel like I was

in my own private Tarzan film. Then, entering the laboratory, I was captivated by the rows and rows of experiments and inventions in various stages of development. To my amazement, several original light bulbs, used ten hours a day since 1925, were still burning.

Our teacher took great pleasure in quoting Mr. Edison, who said, "I will never put my name on any product that is not made to the best of my ability and from the best materials I can produce or buy." This philosophy was clearly acted out in every aspect of Edison's endeavors.

I still remember my childhood impression that Edison's laboratory looked like one giant playroom. It was a far cry from the sterile, uninteresting scene I had conjured up in my young mind.

Years later, as an adult, I went back to Fort Myers and the Edison home, this time with a spirit of enthusiasm and exploration. I wanted to absorb all the inspiration I could. What fascinated me during that second trip was not the inventions themselves; it was the genius that inspired them and the determination that saw them through.

Everything about the Thomas Alva Edison winter home urgently reminds the visitor of Edison's lifelong motto:

Keep at it!

Those three simple words enabled this extraordinary man to become the greatest electrical genius of this century. He was once asked by a news reporter, "Were any of your inventions brilliant intuitions?"

"No," Edison replied, "none of my inventions came by accident. I see a worthwhile need to be met, and I make trial after trial until it comes.

It boils down to
1 percent inspiration
and 99 percent perspiration."

Edison's most profound advice is quoted as "Learn to be a good loser. Never be discouraged when things don't work out—*keep at it!"* And no one would know more about this principle than he did. Edison is said to have collected more than three thousand wild plants and shrubs in his search for rubber plants that would grow in America.

Reportedly, it took four thousand attempts before the light bulb became a reality.

His keep-at-it attitude fueled him to invent not only the bulb, but the sockets, the switches, the wiring, the transmission lines, the meters, and anything else necessary at the time for the use of electricity.

In fact, Edison seemed to delight in improving and expanding his own inventions. He made the first short, silent movies, then he created the first full story on film, "The Great Train Robbery."

But of all Edison's inventions, two particular ones stand out in my mind as the most awe-inspiring: the phonograph and the talking movies. Why those two? Because both involved sound, and Mr. Edison was almost entirely deaf. He was never able to hear those inventions work. How's that for going beyond your own potential?

His friend, James Newton, speaks fondly of a photograph Mr. Edison signed for him with this inscription:

All things come to him
who hustles while he waits.

It is evident Thomas Edison spent a lifetime hustling. His adventurous nature appears to have been even more inspired and motivated when he challenged others to invent the impossible too. Being outdone was never a threat to him. In fact, I think the success of others was fuel for his soul. He just kept working, experimenting, failing, and succeeding.

Henry Ford, no underachiever himself, recounted the story of his first meeting with Thomas Edison as a turning point in his life. After listening to Ford's new-fangled idea with some intensity, Edison banged his fist on the table as he said, "Young man, that's the thing! Your car is self-contained: no boiler, no heavy battery, no smoke or steam. *Keep at it!"*

Ford was amazed that this brilliant, electrical genius would be willing to say that his gas car could be better than an electric car.

That first meeting was the beginning of an intimate friendship between the Fords and the Edisons. Later on, Henry Ford built a home next door to Edison in Fort Myers. The two exchanged inspirations and stories over a lifetime. And it was Henry Ford who gave Edison a check for $750,000 to rebuild his laboratory after a ravaging fire destroyed all the buildings.

We may remember failed attempts in our own lives as monumental disasters, but for Edison, failure was an asset. After nine thousand failed experiments in the creation of a storage battery, his assistants tried to discourage his continuing efforts.

His response: "Failures? Those are not failures. Those are nine thousand things we have learned that won't work, nine thousand things we won't have to do over. We're just that much closer to getting there!"

He strongly believed

Anything
we have the mental capacity
to conceive,
we have the physical ability
to produce.

To Edison, the word *impossible* simply did not exist.

If you look back at your own life with Edison's view, you cannot help but wonder, *could it be that each botched experiment and every miscalculated goal was really a very good thing?*

Fort Myers was my home for a good many years. I made lots and lots of mistakes there, but I also won some great victories, mostly over myself. And now, glancing over my shoulder at what once was, I can see how those adventures in defeat gave me a certain inner strength to go on. After all, when you've already messed up, why not risk it all? Why not attempt to build higher and further into the future? Why not get better at life and at being yourself?

I've thought many times of giving up, but when I do I can almost swear I hear Edison whispering in my ear, *Keep at it!* You haven't yet come anywhere close to discovering nine thousand ways it can't be done!

It is fitting that Fort Myers celebrates the life of its most famous citizen with a yearly extravaganza that draws thousands of visitors from across the country. If you're visiting Florida in February, this is a not-to-be-missed occasion. Beginning on Edison's birthday, February 11, the celebration goes on for two weeks, culminating on Saturday evening with the Festival of Lights Parade, rated as one of the top five night parades in the country.

No wonder the Fort Myers *News Press* chose a statement by Edison as its daily slogan: "There is only one Fort Myers, and ninety million people are going to find it."

Those millions of people have not only discovered Fort Myers, they've also found their imaginations set alight by that brilliant genius, Thomas Alva Edison, Fort Myers's most inspirational native.

17 FORT MYERS BEACH

Bringing in the Treasure

Almost any weekend of the early seventies you could have found me hanging out at Fort Myers Beach—surfing, skimboarding, and looking for fun. Over the years, jet skis and parasailing have been added to the array of enticements there, and the facilities and pavilion have been improved and expanded. But one thing about this beach area never changes: The atmosphere is energized by sun and surf.

Fort Myers Beach is also home to many a shrimp boat. I spent several seasick summers on those rough ships, my wide eyes watching and young ears listening. What I thought was useless information then has turned out to be surprisingly valuable today:

A definite destination makes the difference. Every time the boat headed out to deep water, I thought I would die before we returned. My idea was to stay where it was calm and hope to lure the shrimp in to us. No such luck. Careful calculations took us to the haul we needed.

In life, I've learned that you have to go out where the opportunity is. It won't come swimming in to you.

It costs something to be successful. Sharks and coral tear the nets, causing time-consuming and costly repairs, but the catch is worth the investment.

The smart shrimper stops to **make the repairs as early as possible,** while the rip is small; to ignore it is to invite disaster. The mending means getting up earlier or doing without free time, but *it is essential to success the next time and the next.*

> *Risk and opportunity always bring sacrifice—*
> *giving up to gain.*

This concept runs like a thread throughout the endeavors of life.

The net gain includes treasure and trash. Every time the nets were lowered, they yielded up treasure: exotic shells, lobsters, crabs, and shrimp. But they also brought up trash: sharks, eels, rubber tires, tin cans, and whatever else had been carelessly thrown overboard by boaters. Once the net was emptied onto the deck, the tedious process of deciding what was waste and what is of value began.

> *Quite simply, this relates to the setting of priorities*
> *in our lives: Who or what gets our best?*

Once you begin, don't turn back. Many days I found myself lying on the bow of the boat, praying we'd miraculously turn around and head for home. I knew I was dreaming, though. As far as the shrimpers are concerned, once you begin the voyage, there's no turning back until the posted date.

No matter what you're doing, it is imperative that you finish what you start regardless of the circumstances or lack of comfort. Some of the grandest wins have come when a strong competitor gave up just a second too soon.

Sometimes several boats went out at the same time, but only one would come back with an extraordinary haul. I asked the captain about this once and he said "Jay, you never know what gifts the tide will bestow upon you. But one thing is sure—if I don't go out and drop the net, I'm guaranteed to haul in nothing. It's sure worth the try."

Now ain't *that* the truth?

18 CAPE CORAL

Waterfront Wonderland

Take 104-plus square miles of flat wasteland, swamps, palmetto scrubs, and cattle pastures; add more than five hundred miles of winding, man-made canals and a variety of pastel, stucco houses dotted with swimming pools and boat docks. Blend this together and you have the "Waterfront Wonderland" known as Cape Coral.

The growth continues to explode as more and more people are attracted to the young, affordable city. Because vacant lots at inexpensive prices are plentiful, many people find they can afford a boat or a bigger house when they move here.

But before you break ground on a new house, be sure to check for burrowing owls. These endangered friends can be seen any day, basking in the Florida sun, oblivious to their nocturnal relatives. Burrowing deep into the sand, they establish their nests, and state law gives them prior ownership rights until they move voluntarily.

Cape Coral is connected to its sister city, Fort Myers, by a bridge, and the view of the Caloosahatchee River as you enter the city is spectacular. An array of boats speckles the vast river with color, tempting the driver to abandon the common mode of travel for the thrill of a speedboat or the hypnotic lull of a sailboat. Astonishing as it seems, you can take the intercoastal waterway—across the Caloosahatchee to Lake Okeechobee, through Palm Beach to the Atlantic Ocean—without ever setting foot on land.

Once you're across the toll bridge, make a few turns and you'll arrive at the public beach, which features a screened pavilion, a 620-foot fishing pier, and well-maintained facilities. Presiding over the beach area is the stately Cape Coral Yacht and Racquet Club. With its huge event hall, docking facilities, tennis courts, a senior recreation center, and Olympic-size pool complete with a high-diving board and two regulation boards, its facilities are available to tourists for a nominal fee.

For me, Cape Coral is more than just another destination on our tour of the Sunshine State. I still enjoy fond memories of my wife, Diane, and I riding a tandem bike throughout the town during our courtship more than twenty years ago. Her wonderful, warm Italian family still lives there, and I have learned a great deal about love from them. Her dad, Joe Raso, is an amazing man, and I have gleaned a great deal of wisdom from his life.

More than half a century ago, as a young man of fifteen, Joe traveled with his mother and sister by ship from Italy to New York, pursuing the promise of opportunity. By necessity, income ruled over education so he was forced to drop out of school. Instead, Joe taught himself English by reading the dictionary over and over. He worked hard and saved until he was finally able to open his own bar and grill in a small town outside Pittsburgh, Pennsylvania. It was the American dream fulfilled.

Life was good. Business was good. Then one day, as he fondly recalls, a salesman came into the bar with some slick brochures on a new city in Florida. "It's called Cape Coral—it's a waterfront wonderland!" the man said. The very name spoke of faraway adventure.

Joe took the information, thanked the man, and went back to work. In the back of his mind, however, he kept remembering the childhood thrill of venturing across the ocean toward the unknown. By now he had four daughters and a fifth child on the way. The Rasos' relatives and friends lived in a neighborhood where no one was a stranger, at least not for long. Everything seemed to be going so well, but that adventurous word *wonderland* kept popping into his mind.

It wasn't long until Joe gave up his comfortable life and gave in to his dream of starting over once again in yet another new land. He sold it all, packed his bags, and headed for a new life in Cape Coral. His first job was as a bartender making the same salary per week that his own restaurant had grossed in one day. Still, he was excited enough about this new beginning to give it all he had.

Within a few months, his wife, Grace, drove the four girls and her ailing father-in-law from Pennsylvania to Florida in the family station wagon. (Did I mention she was seven months pregnant at the time?) It was quite a trip—the travelers found themselves in the midst of Hurricane Donna that swept through Georgia where they stopped overnight. Grace says she prayed through the night for safety, all the while questioning the venture away from the familiar.

Substitute "station wagon" for "covered wagon" and I think you can get an authentic picture of these courageous twentieth-century pioneers. Finally the trip was over as they drove the last stretch into Cape Coral.

As Grace recalls it, nothing could have been more emotionally draining than that trip across the Edison Bridge. In the aftermath of the hurricane, which had also devastated Florida, broken glass covered the walkways, downed power lines dangled from their supports, trees were strewn across roadways, and ditches were overrun with what looked like swamp water. As she searched for the right address, Grace hoped against hope that this wasn't really the place Joe had written home about with such enthusiasm.

With his usual optimistic smile, Joe welcomed Grace. "This is our land of opportunity, our new beginning," he told her. Not sure what to think, she forced a smile. She remembers thinking, *It's OK. He'll be ready to go back soon.*

In the meantime Joe set about building their dream home. He was confident of the future and in unlimited opportunity— as long as everyone worked hard for it.

Always the self-starter, he set out to learn the real estate business and soon began convincing other adventurous souls from "up North" and even from his native Italy to come to the waterfront wonderland of Cape Coral. With the Webster's Dictionary as his English tutor, Joe Raso moved up from bartender to salesman, then soon became a sales-closer, was promoted to office manager and then to area manager. Eventually he opened his own real estate office—Raso Realty.

His dream of a new beginning began to take shape as the little town of "nowhere" built new bridges, a hospital, retail stores, various social clubs and halls, and continued to thrive.

Some thirty years after that first slick brochure tantalized him with adventure Raso Realty continues to introduce visitors and curiosity seekers to Cape Coral real estate. Stop by the office on Cape Coral Street and say hello to two of Joe's daughters, who now run the business. (Tell them Jay sent you!) And don't miss their newest venture—Razzle Dazzle, where you'll find unique, Florida-style clothing at its best.

Joe and Grace still live in their canal-front dream home, now affectionately called "Gracie's on the Water." On almost any Sunday, you can smell the aroma of homemade bread and hear the laughter of grandchildren playing there in confirmation of "the good life."

Joe Raso's story reminds me of a poem by Edgar A. Guest. In fact, it makes me wonder if young students in Italy might have been studying it some fifty years ago!

It Couldn't Be Done

Somebody said that it couldn't be done
But he with a chuckle replied
That maybe it couldn't, but he would be one
Who wouldn't say so till he tried.
So he buckled right in with the trace of grin
On his face. If he worried, he hid it.
He started to sing as he tackled the thing
That couldn't be done, and he did it.
Somebody scoffed: "Oh, you'll never do that;
At least no one ever has done it."
But he took off his coat and took off his hat
And the first thing he knew he'd begun it.
With the lift of his chin and a bit of a grin,
Without any doubting or quiddit,
He started to sing as he tackled the thing
That couldn't be done, and he did it.
There are thousands to tell you it cannot be done,
There are thousands to prophesy failure;
There are thousands to point out to you, one by one,
The dangers that wait to assail you.
But just buckle right in with a bit of a grin,
Then take off your coat and go to it;
Just start in to sing as you tackle the thing
That "cannot be done"—and you'll do it.

Ask my father-in-law about risk, sacrifice, and opportunity, and he'll tell you the truth, spoken from the soul of a Florida pioneer: "Yes, go for it. Always follow your dreams. Hard work and a loving family will take you where you want to go."

19 SANIBEL AND CAPTIVA

Get Up Early If You Want the Best

The gulf coast beaches of Florida are well known, but Sanibel and Captiva stand out among them as uniquely idyllic islands. A drive across the drawbridge transports you into a simpler time.

Just one mile wide and twelve miles long, Sanibel has been declared one of the three best shell-collecting spots in the world. It is an island intent on preserving its relaxed ambience as well as the sanctity of the environment.

Lazy bike rides along shaded trails, canoe trips through the Ding Darling National Wildlife Refuge, the view from the lighthouse point, a seascape dotted with sailboats, and dinner at the Bubble Room at Captiva are among my favorite memories of this place. Alligators soaking up the sun on the golf course greens are frequent guests. Just smile at them and go the other way.

This is one of my favorite sabbatical spots. And when I'm vacationing, the first and foremost rule for those who know me well is a timeless one: Don't wake me or you die! I am a night person, a lover of the moon and the stillness of darkness. I love to read late into the wee hours, to study, to spend quiet hours restoring my soul. Of course the result of my nocturnal wakefulness is that if you rouse me early on my days off, I'm like a roaring lion, growling as I go.

The ocean is my passion, and I often recline on the hotel balcony to relax, play games with the family, or read while overlooking the sea. One particular evening after the rest of the family had gone to bed, I reveled in the solitude, enjoying the sound of the surf playing in the background. It was so peaceful that I actually fell asleep in the chaise. The lullaby of the ocean encouraged my slumber, and I am sure I dreamed of faraway sailing ships and adventures.

I was awakened by a subtle change in the darkness. It was not yet daybreak; the sun had not risen, but it was lighter nonetheless. I sat up, rubbed my eyes, and surveyed the horizon. At first all seemed calm. But then an unusual display of little light beams dancing about the beach caught my attention. Rubbing my eyes again, I strained to find the source of those rays. As the rising sun slowly revealed the answer I couldn't help but chuckle.

Dozens of people with flashlights strapped to their heads were searching and combing the beach for rare shells. *These*, I thought, *are* serious *collectors!*

"The early bird gets the worm" is a common phrase, but flashlights and beachcombing before dawn? Well, maybe they were onto something. Andrew Carnegie once said

> *The first man gets the oyster.*
> *The second man gets only an empty shell.*

In this case, the shell appeared to be the main prize! I *had* to investigate. I arrived at the beach as the sun was rising—a breathtaking sight, almost worth getting up early for. (I'll continue to settle for the beauty of a sunset, however.) Trying to blend in, I mingled with the others, scavenging the shore.

Out of nowhere, a woman approached me with a broad smile: "A spectacular find! But you're too late. All that's left are the scraps."

Hmmm, now where have I heard those words before?

We live in the day of "get there first, and get it done fast." Technology has blessed us with an assortment of efficiency devices such as microwaves to speed the cooking process from hours to minutes, facsimile machines to send letters in seconds instead of days, and computers to store and retrieve files instantly. The whole idea is to go faster and save time.

But as the availability of timesavers multiplies, so does the length of our "to do" list. We scurry down hallways, glancing at our watches, exclaiming, "I'm late, I'm late!" like the white rabbit hurrying to a date in Wonderland. Time is such a precious, rationed commodity that if it were available for purchase it would cause Americans to line up around the block, desperate to buy it.

Personally, I think time management is only the beginning of organizing life. The setting of priorities comes first. For years Sears has been advertising three classes of products: good, better, and best. When it comes to priorities, most of us choose "good" because we never take the time to determine what is "best." Maybe we should consider what our "best" priorities should be. Here are some I've chosen for myself.

Priority in energy. The shell-seeking woman I met on the beach chose to give up sleep in order to find what she wanted. I have sole control over who or what I choose to give my best energy to. Until I exercise this control, energy will be robbed from me at every turn and I will have no say-so over the distribution of it. In my life my list of energy priorities—simple and unchanging—is:

1. My faith

2. My family

3. My work

4. My church and friends

Priority in decision-making. Who feels like getting up before dawn? I only feel like working out after I've watched a *Rocky* movie! Feelings are wonderful directionals when they happen to be positive and on target, but they are great distracters—even deceivers—when they're not. Emotions can build us up or tear us down. If I based my self-image on my emotions, I'd feel like a million dollars one day and small change the next!

Making the *best* decisions every day and for the future takes decisiveness, determination, and dogged persistence—no matter how I "feel."

Priority in motive. The value of seashells is in the eye of the one who collects them. While there are some industries and cultures who incorporate the use of shells into useful products, the average collector selects them for their sheer beauty. Their motive is pure pleasure.

How simple and uncomplicated my motives are when I work for the joy of a job well done:

- I don't do things because I have to, but because I want to.

- I don't want something because my friend has it, but because it means something to me to own it.

- I don't try things because of what others will think of me if I succeed, but for the enjoyment I will receive from giving it my best.

Am I encountering disappointment because someone else has succeeded and I haven't? If so, I have to reexamine my motives. If I have pure motives, I view failure as a valuable map that will help me find my way along the road to success.

Priority in resources. One thing I remember well from my boyhood days aboard shrimp boats: The prettiest shell or souvenir of the sea can smell as foul as a rotten fish if it's not cleaned and preserved properly. I recall hiding a beautiful starfish in my bunk, hoping to keep it for myself. It wasn't very long before I threw it overboard—it was smelling up the whole boat. I couldn't properly preserve the starfish, and it became unbearable to everyone.

- Doctors report that 50 percent of diseases have stress as a primary root or symptom. What are we doing to preserve our health?

- Statistics tell us that 50 percent of marriages end in divorce. What are we doing to preserve our families?

- Lawsuits among former business partners are at an all-time high. What are we doing to preserve our relationships?

In trying to preserve what we have, we sometimes fight too hard to keep it in our possession. We seek peace of mind by attempting to control all the elements of our lives. But in doing so we drive ourselves (and everyone around us) crazy in our efforts to keep everything under control!

As a young lad about to be married, a wise southern preacher gave me this advice: "Young man, always save a tenth, give away a tenth, and live on the rest. You'll make it just fine." I was skeptical of this advice, but I have experienced its validity firsthand over the years.

Give, and it shall be given to you.

This is wisdom with promise.

Priority in our values. "She Sells Sea Shells" is a retail store in Sanibel for those of us who don't make it to the beach early. I've bought some beautiful specimens there. But when house guests ask me where I "found" them, I've learned there isn't much glamour in replying "Oh, I bought them at a shop in town."

If what you have
has cost you little,
it will be of little value to others.

Hyrum W. Smith, CEO of Franklin Quest, begins his seminars by helping people identify what he calls their "governing principles." He has them write out a statement describing and defining them. To quote Smith: "Once you know what you value, you make better use of your time."

It's like the road to Sanibel, I guess. It requires a toll, but the price is small in comparison to the rich, exotic treasures that await you there.

Getting the best, being the best, and preserving the best are always worth the price.

20 SARASOTA-VENICE

Once upon a Child

I can still hear the barkers: "Ladies and gentlemen! Step right up! Get your tickets to the Greatest Show on Earth!"

The Greatest Show on Earth—they said it, and I believed it! Nothing could match the drama and excitement of going to the circus. Daredevil acts were my favorites, and I dreamed of becoming a lion tamer. Even today, I don't miss a chance to visit Sarasota, a fun-loving, circus-minded town, and Venice, the birthplace of the circus.

In Sarasota, the Circus Galleries continue to celebrate Tom Thumb, Emmett Kelly, and other big-top legends with photographs, posters, and memorabilia of circus days. If you stay long enough, you may find yourself hearing a distant calliope or catching the whiff of cotton candy.

On the more serious side, the John and Mable Ringling Museum of Art is world-famous for its rare fine-art collections. Some have even called it "the Louvre of Florida" because of its treasured paintings and historic tapestries.

And if all of this isn't enough, take a stroll through Ringling's palace, the Ca'd'Zan, the House of John. Built in 1926 at a cost of 1.5 million dollars—before furnishings—the word *elaborate* just doesn't do it justice.

Just down the road is Venice, the winter home of the Ringling Brothers and Barnum and Bailey Circus. When they arrive here, this is "down time" for the performers: wounds are healed, sets are redesigned and repaired, and shows are rehearsed. Then, in a magnificent debut, a public premier of the newest season's "star-studded spectacular" is held every year in late December.

The Clown College is also in Venice. Here a unique assortment of students learn to juggle, walk on stilts, and put on clown makeup. Most of all, they learn how to make people laugh and have fun. It is the world's only school devoted exclusively to the art of clowning.

I meet people every day, and I'm sure you do, too, who could definitely use a refresher course from this particular academy. Day after day in the hectic pace of deadlines, solving problems, and recovering from hurt feelings, some of us have forgotten the simple joy of a good laugh.

Medical science has freely admitted the therapeutic value of touch and laughter in combating the elusive but very real influence of stressful living. When Peter Pan instructed Wendy to "think happy thoughts," he was giving her a wise and effective prescription.

The uneasy feeling in the pit of your stomach could be the child inside wanting to get out and play. How long has it been since you've really had *fun?* Think about it.

At one time or another, every one of us struggles with

- Fatigue

- Frustration

- Fault-finders

- Fear

- Failure.

Maybe at least a partial antidote for these poisons is another simple little word:

- FUN!

We constantly hear about watching what we eat. I think the real danger lies elsewhere. What's eating *you?* Life's simple pleasures have been replaced with worry and anxiety. Stress captures our hearts and holds us hostage. Called by some doctors the fastest-growing disease in the world, stress is said to be responsible for 50 percent of illnesses in hospitals today.

My friend Gary Carter is one of the best catchers ever to play major-league baseball. In eleven all-star games, he was twice voted Most Valuable Player. Gary has had two-thousand-plus hits, scored one thousand runs, and has twelve hundred RBIs. He led the New York Mets to the world championship in 1986 and has consistently given 100 percent in every game, even when playing with an injury.

I remember talking with Gary during some difficult days, when a temporary slump kept him from that "magic number" of runs. Realizing that burnout occurs in the inner spirit, he kept the self-talk going and continued to have faith in himself. Game after game, he gave it his best shot until the victory day came.

Gary Carter is serious about his game, but he is just as earnest about having fun.

Nicknamed "The Kid" by teammates and the media, Gary claps, whoops, and hollers about professional baseball just like he did in his Little League days. With the joy of a child and the seriousness of a professional, Gary Carter is a winner on and off the field.

Kids may be in a hurry to grow up, but adults long for "the good old days" when they were children. Americans spend billions of dollars every year on *amusements*. This is an interest-ing word: "muse" means to think, but when preceded by an "a" it changes to "not to think." In an effort to escape the wear and tear of living, we look for ways to occupy our minds with en-tertainment.

As a little girl, my daughter Christa asked on a cross-coun-try trip, "Dad, when we get there will we be where we're go-ing?" Pretty intelligent question when you think about it! If we have no definite destination we end up wherever the road or the crowd may lead.

Whatever goals we set, we owe it to ourselves to approach them with maturity, enthusiasm, and excitement, which just might be the energy source for our determination and dedica-tion. But why not have some fun along the way? Let's try to live life with all the determination and dedication of a grown-up and the enthusiasm and energy of a kid at the circus!

21 SAINT PETERSBURG- CLEARWATER

Bloom Where You're Planted

When I was a kid, I was convinced that Granny grew the prettiest orchids in Florida. Even as a nine-year-old boy intent on playing in the dirt and staying away from silly girls, I was drawn to her fragile, fragrant flowers. It was a mystery to me how Granny could make those beautiful lavender-and-white blooms keep appearing out of drab, clay pots. On the other side of the orange grove, Granddad raised all kinds of vegetables and fruits. The growth process seemed like magic to my young mind, and I often followed both of them around asking questions.

Since those days I have had the opportunity to speak and vacation in the St. Petersburg-Clearwater area several times.

Clearwater is fitly named for its beautiful beaches and clear waters. I have a keen interest in its Marine Science Center, which is dedicated to the rescue, treatment, and release of marine mammals and sea turtles. In St. Pete, I make it a point to roam through the surreal art of the Salvador Dali Museum. But it is St. Petersburg's splendid Sunken Gardens that I especially enjoy.

It's hard to imagine a grander garden than this jungle-like paradise. Tropical birds and various kinds of wildlife thrive among fifty thousand exotic plants, giving the impression of a native rain forest. A vivid variety of flowers, including thousands of rare orchids, bloom year-round. The result is a brilliant palette of color painted like a horizontal rainbow across the vast acreage. And every bloom reminds me of Granny's orchids and Granddad's gardens.

The story of the gardens' origin has remained with me through the years. Believe it or not the fertile, flourishing bounty of beauty was once a soggy, useless crater. Originally a sinkhole, landscaping now lends beauty to the homely hole.

Doesn't life feel like that sometimes? It seems empty and unproductive. You find yourself in the midst of situations and environments that are unchangeable, at least for the time being. As Oliver Wendell Holmes once said,

> **The great thing in the world**
> **is not so much in where we stand**
> **as in what direction we are moving.**

Two options open their doors: Sink into stagnant waters or bloom where you're planted. It's hard work, but I'll choose plants and landscaping anytime!

Most of Granny's gardening hints have long strayed from memory, but I do remember one. She said the most important thing is to cultivate the beds. In Granny language: "If you don't get the soil ready *before* you plant, you can't expect it to produce anything *after* you plant." Makes sense to me. To *cultivate* is to prepare the soil by breaking it up, moving out of our stagnant comfort zone.

Once you've made the commitment to bloom, it changes the way you view your future. You no longer stare down the road, longing for unavailable options. Instead, you look at the street you are on, and you check the map frequently to verify that you are headed in the right direction. You understand that sacrifices today will benefit you tomorrow. The decision to grow as a person and even to bloom provides a new perspective for life's circumstances.

- For a marriage on the rocks, it means making the decision to try. *Concentrate on improving yourself no matter what your mate does.*

- In a difficult work situation, it speaks positive self-talk: *I don't work for a boss—I work for myself.* Every skill, experience, and bit of knowledge takes you closer to success.

- During a financial slump, some things are beyond your control. *Put your energy into what you can change.* Rejoice in your positive successes and the good things in your life such as your family and friendships.

- When a new idea seems stalled, it tells you: *Keep on tilling until you've produced at least one bloom.* That way you will have a positive keepsake to motivate you, no matter what you decide to do.

One of the most insightful examples of blooming where you're planted comes from a tale of French prisoners of war during World War II. The prisoners were forced to work in a German munitions factory. Upon realizing that the very bombs they were building were being used to destroy their beloved homeland, they made the decision to create a malfunction in the detonation.

On impact the bombs were harmless—no explosion occurred. Puzzled by so many failed attacks, the French government conducted an investigation. Upon opening the bombs, they found slips of paper inside bearing these words:

*We are doing the best we can
with what we've got,
where we are,
every chance we get.*

Remember that a garden never leaves the plot of ground where it began. Yet all who venture through it are inspired, and they take its beauty and fragrance away with them. You will always have an impact on those in your garden or circle of influence—no matter the size or location.

P.S. To all of you who live in the St. Petersburg-Tampa Bay area: Major League Baseball owes you a team. You have tilled the ground, planted and watered the seeds, and now it is time to harvest the crop. Play ball!

22 TAMPA

Patriots and Pirates, the Takers and the Givers

Tampa offers a variety of attractions to the tourist, ranging from amusement parks to pirate parades as well as the colorful Cuban quarter of Ybor City. The downtown area boasts a growing port for various cruise lines, and it doesn't end there. The entire port area is undergoing revitalization as the 20.5-acre Garrison Seaport Center begins to take shape along the waterfront.

An eighty-four-million-dollar aquarium with a three-level dome and an eighty-foot-high glass roof in the shape of a seashell is schedule to open in 1995. Sounds spectacular, doesn't it?

Tampa is well known for its annual Gasparilla parade, a celebration of its pirate days in the past. The legend and lore of adventurous pirates are modified a bit in order to change their history from evil to "naughty, but romantic." And the fantasy of swashbuckling pirates has been the backdrop for great fun and revelry in Tampa for more than seventy years.

As for Tampa's pirate, José Gaspar (he changed his name to Gasparilla when he left the Spanish navy), legend has it the pirate jumped overboard and drowned himself by wrapping a heavy chain around his waist. His treasures were never discovered, and he left behind nothing but multi-hued sagas.

As a boy, pirates tales loomed bigger than life in my imagination. One moment I imagined myself with an eye patch, a wooden leg, and an arm hook—I was the pirate who wouldn't die. The next moment, I was a crew hand forced to walk the plank and be drowned in the sea. Either way the daydream was an exciting escapade of adventure without ever leaving my room!

Less celebrated but still of great fame are the many courageous patriots of American history who have lived in and around Tampa. Indeed, the city has been fortunate to host both heroes and heroines.

So . . . rummaging through the dusty artifacts of Tampa's history we discover usable salvage spun into colorful tales of pirates and patriots. These represent the two basic types of people we can choose to become: pirates, who epitomize the takers, and patriots, who portray the givers.

Just for a moment, let's realistically read of the eighteenth- and nineteenth-century pirates. Phrases like "bloodthirsty, lustful, heartless, and slavemongers" are peppered throughout history books in describing their behavior. They were greedy, savage thieves, takers of anything or anyone they desired. Their legendary plundering is too vast to document.

Takers are rude, belittling, and selfish. It all begins with the individual's view of mankind.

- Takers view others as objects: "What's yours is mine, and I'll take it."

Totally on the opposite side are the givers. They are gracious, encouraging, and self-sacrificing.

- Givers appreciate people as opportunities: "What's mine is mine, but I'll share it."

Such is the case for the three patriots I would like to focus on. As you will see, their own words identify them as givers in sharp contrast to the deeds of the pirate/taker. Their intent was to significantly make a difference in the world through sacrifice of themselves. They are Theodore Roosevelt, Francis Bellamy, and H. Norman Schwarzkopf. All three have strong ties to Tampa and the surrounding area.

President Theodore Roosevelt was a colonel in the United States Army during the Spanish-American War when some thirty thousand were encamped in the Tampa-Lakeland area. The Tampa Bay Hotel served as camp headquarters, and Colonel Roosevelt trained his Rough Riders on the surrounding grounds. He was often seen riding his horse through the environs of Tampa.

The memorable quotations of this Tampa soldier are bountiful, but I have chosen just a few that I believe show his spirit of giving and commitment to his country.

"Far and away the best prize that life offers is the chance to work hard at work worth doing."

"No man is justified in doing evil on the ground of expediency."

"No man is worth his salt who is not ready at all times to risk his body, to risk his well-being, to risk his life, in a great cause."

"In any moment of decision the best thing you can do is the right thing, the next best thing is the wrong thing, and the worst thing you can do is nothing."

"Aggressive fighting for the right is the greatest sport in the world."

The **Francis Bellamy** school in Tampa was named for the author of the "Pledge of Allegiance." He was a Baptist minister who worked in Tampa in the 1920s. His words will, of course, continue in our hearts for generations to come.

*I pledge allegiance to the flag
of the United States of America,
and to the republic for which it stands;
one nation, under God, indivisible,
with liberty and justice for all.*

Now retired and living in Tampa, **General H. Norman Schwarzkopf** was a household word during the Persian Gulf War. Highly acclaimed for his strategies of leadership and winning, he was nicknamed the "People's General" because of his communication skills during Gulf War military briefings. General Schwarzkopf's reputation is synonymous with honesty and integrity; most of the following Schwarzkopf quotes are taken from his autobiography, *It Doesn't Take a Hero.*

"The truth of the matter is that you always know the right thing to do. The hard part is doing it."

"Never lie, ever. It undermines your credibility."

"'Duty, honor, country' was [his father's] *creed, and it became mine."*

"It doesn't take a hero to order men into battle. It takes a hero to be one of those men who goes into battle."

"Be known as an individual who can deliver; don't wing it, no false bravado."

"Always have a worst-case scenario prepared for every situation."

"The better informed a soldier is the better he fights."

"I don't fix blame, I fix problems."

"Don't win the war and lose the peace."

Although these patriots lived during separate epochs in American history, and different circumstances confronted them, they shared a common goal: to make a difference in the history of their beloved country. They leave behind a wealthy heritage of tenacity in fighting for the good and just cause.

As patriots, they are beloved examples—givers, not takers—in world that is all too plentiful with pirates, even today.

23 SPOOK HILL

The Illusion of Fear

Listening to Mom read the brochure, I thought, *Sure. Right. You sit on level ground and roll backwards, all the while thinking you're headed forward. Is this a desperate attempt at tourism, or what?*

She read on . . .

In ancient days, an Indian village on Lake Wales was plagued by an incredibly large and vicious alligator. The village chief was a brave, fearless warrior who took it upon himself to confront and battle the dangerous tormenter. The fierce fight between them resulted in the tragic death of both the warrior and the gator.

To this day, legend has it, the ghost of the Indian chief restlessly haunts the land, angry over the intrusion of modern times into his village.

Others believe the ghost of the alligator haunts the area in its hunger for revenge.

No one knows for sure what really happened, but for years, horses have been spooked and wagons overtaken by strange occurrences in this locale, incidents that defy all explanation. An unknown ghost continues to live at what is now known as Spook Hill.

Okay, I thought to myself, staring at Mom's face for a clue, *maybe this did happen hundreds of years ago, but it's not going to happen today. Technology and knowledge make stories like this obsolete.*

Still, some little spark of adventure inside me had set my curiosity aflame. I found myself climbing into the car with anticipation. Soon Mom was driving down US 27 and then heading off the beaten path to Spook Hill.

In disbelief I watched her drive to the designated spot and park the car. We quickly jumped out to investigate. The land looked level enough; in fact, it was downright flat. I got back in, put the gear in neutral, and waited cynically. "This can't work. What in the world are these people talking about?" I said.

Then I realized the car was moving.

At first, I blamed it on an optical illusion, but the car was picking up speed as it rolled backward. And yet we were parked on level ground. Weren't we? As if that weren't enough, each time I glanced into the rearview mirror, I became queasy. In the mirror, it looked as if we were moving *forward.*

I can't believe this. Is there really a ghost, or is this the product of a vivid imagination on a lonely road?

Even though I was in no danger, the eeriness of the moment caused me to feel afraid. And that fear felt familiar. How many times had I faced the unknown, only to find it had no power of its own? My fear was fueled only by my own apprehensions, not by any real threat.

I wish I had known then what I have finally learned as an adult: An overwhelming majority of our fears never come to pass. For years I have depended on this definition of FEAR to help me overcome it:

False

Evidence that

Appears

Real

Motivational speaker Mamie McCullough, my good friend, says it this way:

> *I know that worry works*
> *because almost everything I worry about*
> *ends up not coming true!*

Unfortunately some people live on their own personal Spook Hills. Fear and worry have become a way of life for too many of them. The word *worry* comes from an old English term meaning "to strangle," and it will quite literally choke the life out of your future. Along similar lines, the word *anxious* means to be torn apart. Dr. John Maxwell teaches:

> *If there is no faith in the future,*
> *there can be no power in the present.*

Perhaps that is the reason the Bible says "Fear not" 365 times, one for each day of the year. The doorway to our dreams for the future is often blocked by barricades of fear. Before us stands an ultimatum of three choices:

Faint in depression. To forfeit a game for any reason is an automatic loss for a team. The worst consequence of forfeiture is never knowing whether you could have won the game after all. For us to give up is to live in a chronic state of wondering what might have happened if we'd gone on.

Gus D'Amato, the renowned trainer of boxing champions, revealed great wisdom when he observed,

> *Heroes and cowards*
> *feel exactly the same fear;*
> *heroes just react differently.*

Flee in cowardice. To run from fear may at first appear logical, but it is a never-ending race. Every day that fear will hunt us down again, always lurking just over our shoulder, ever gaining on us and overshadowing every decision. Eleanor Roosevelt was an extraordinary woman who knew firsthand the merit of courage. She once stated,

> *You gain strength, courage, and confidence*
> *by every experience when you must*
> *stop and look fear in the face.*
> *You must do the thing you think you cannot do.*

When I was in the seventh grade, a boy named Dennis Norman hit me square in the mouth during an after-school fight. Horrified by the blood streaming down my chin, I ran away and quit after that first punch. Later, hiding in my room, the grim truth came to me: The punch in the mouth hurt a whole lot less than the sick feeling in my heart after running away from a fight.

Fight to overcome. One very significant book, *The Conquest of Fear* by Basil King, has stood the test of time. In it, the author offers this advice:

> *Go at it boldly*
> *and you will find unexpected forces*
> *closing round and coming to your aid.*

Emerson wrote:

> *Do the thing you fear and the death of fear is certain.*

And beloved American sage Mark Twain so eloquently said,

> *Courage is resistance to fear,*
> *mastery of fear,*
> *not absence of fear.*

During World War II, a military governor profusely praised George Patton for his gallant and courageous acts. The general replied with a swallow. "Sir, I am not a brave man. The truth of the matter is I am usually a coward at heart. I have never been in the sound of gunshot or sight of battle in my whole life that I was not afraid. I constantly have sweat on my palms and a lump in my throat."

In later years, Patton penned these words:

> *I learned very early in life*
> *not to take counsel of my fears.*

Confront fear's potency with bravery, and you will find it greatly diminished. After all, it's up to you and me to make the decision, changing . . .

- *Worry* into *Willingness*

- *Anxiety* into *Anticipation*

- *"Oh no!"* into *"Oh Yeah!*

- *Spook Hill* into *Courage Mountain!*

24 BOK TOWER

An Attitude of Gratitude

Do you ever feel like you just can't deal with the things that need to be done? Are you lacking the strength to face today's responsibilities? Like a fine, handmade clock, the human spirit can run down and require rewinding or maybe even resetting. The Creator Himself rested after six days of toil, setting an example for us and providing a divine prescription for humankind's well-being.

Sometimes when I find myself weighed down under a burden of stress, I make my way to the gardens of the Bok Tower, located just north of Lake Wales near the intersection of highways 60 and 27. In doing so, I reflect on John Burroughs's comment, "I come here to find myself; it is so easy to get lost in the world." These last words echo the cry of countless hearts. Here, amid 130 acres of azaleas, camellias, magnolias, and countless other exotic blossoms, many souls have "found" themselves.

The sights, sounds, and smells of the gardens awaken my senses and restore my soul. Sitting in the midst of cascading colors and calmness, I feel a stirring within my heart. The verse from Psalm 46:10 seems at this moment to have been written just for me:

Be still
and know that I am God.

Wandering about with no specific agenda is a delight in itself. In the midst of the gardens I encounter the impressive Bok Tower, carved of pink Georgia marble and gray Florida coquina stone. A Florida theme dominates the tower with stone sculptures of wildlife, pelicans, flamingos, ducks, and swans.

The tower houses a carillon of fifty-seven tuned bronze bells, the smallest weighing seventeen pounds and the largest weighing eleven tons. This gives the tower the nickname "Singing Tower," and a reflection pool adorned with graceful swans and ducks surrounds it. The entrance doorway is made of thirty brass panels depicting the Creation story right up to man's expulsion from the garden. Standing here, one feels so at home; surely man was made to live in a garden and to commune with his Creator.

The story behind this oasis cries out to be told. Edward Bok said he came to this country as "a little Dutch boy unceremoniously set down in America, unable to make myself understood or to understand the speech of others. My education was practically nil, yet my destiny was to become the editor of the *Ladies' Home Journal,* at that time the largest-circulation magazine in the world."

Bok was a boy rooted in disadvantage who believed at a young age that, "in America one can do anything as long as it is honest."

I left the Singing Tower with these lasting impressions:

Cultivate an attitude of gratitude. In 1923, Bok purchased a homely, barren sand dune, originally named "Iron Mountain" by the natives. Its transformation into one of the world's most beautiful and acclaimed gardens was performed out of sheer gratitude. The dedication plaque reveals Bok's endeavor of thanksgiving with these words: "Given to the American people." A powerful principle is evident here: Just as gratitude turned a barren dune into a flourishing shrine of tranquility, so gratitude can turn a barren life into a fruitful one.

Set aside time for renewal of the inner man. The most wonderful thing about the Bok Tower is that it requires nothing. There is nothing "to do" at this attraction. The only activities possible are meditation, relaxation, and enjoyment of the gorgeous natural surroundings. It reminds me that

We ought to learn
the incomparable value
of "being"
instead of "doing."

Make the world a better place. As a young lad, Bok's grandmother told him, "Make the world a better or more beautiful place because you have lived in it." This became the mission statement of his life as he vowed to never use the words "that will do" or "it's good enough."

Not many of us have the available resources to establish an elaborate shrine of gratitude, but we can all commit ourselves to making a difference in our own daily walk of life. Our efforts will be appreciated for generation after generation.

Whatever you do with your life, make it count. Clearly, Edward Bok believed in destiny. He did not pretend that any part of his life, from poor immigrant to successful businessman, was a coincidence. He remained focused on his dreams and steadfast in his purpose.

Recently, I read with interest the results of a survey given to fifty people over the age of ninety by sociologist Dr. Tony Campolo. These are the three most consistent answers to the question, "If you could live your life over again, what would you do differently?"

1. *I would reflect more.*

2. *I would risk more.*

3. *I would do more to leave a legacy to pass on after I'm gone.*

The power of a refreshed spirit can energize us in the long haul as well as throughout each day. Although others seek to define success from the *outside-in*, let's try to find our significance from the *inside-out*. An attitude of gratitude is the first step.

25 OCALA

The Will to Win

Do the names *Affirmed, Northern Dancer, Seattle Slew,* and *Secretariat* sound familiar? As you've probably guessed, those monikers identify some of the most outstanding thoroughbred horses in racing history. There are more than six hundred horse farms in the state of Florida, and three-fourths of them are located near Ocala. Besides being home to the fascinating natural wonder of Silver Springs, gushing forth 500 million gallons of crystalline water a day (which you can experience by glass-bottomed boat), the Ocala area has become famous for its thoroughbred horses.

If you take time to drive down the Ocala area's lazy back roads, you'll see stately Arabians grazing under bowing trees— trees heavily laden with Spanish moss. There's enough pretty scenery around to fill dozens of souvenir postcard racks.

I spent an afternoon at one of the picturesque horse farms, and it was more beautiful than I had imagined. What seemed like natural, verdant green meadows turned out to be a high quality of specially developed grass, a particular type that is largely responsible for the health and splendid appearance of the animals. Nature also plays a major role in the horses' well-being by purifying local waters through layers of limestone, thus supplying valuable mineral supplements to the race horses. This combination of fine grass and mineral water does seem to work wonders—at last count, Ocala farms have yielded five Kentucky Derby winners.

The horse-breeding business is a multibillion-dollar industry, but even intense training and the purest of breeding cannot ensure success. In fact, 95 percent of all thoroughbreds never make it as far as the racetrack. Obviously, there is more to being a winner than lineage, careful nutrition, and grooming.

The trainers and owners I've talked with tell me *it's the heart of the horse that counts.* A winning horse is born to run, and it runs to win. Some horses have the pedigree and the proper training, but they are intimidated by the crowd. Others simply never live up to their potential because the desire to win lies untapped within them.

The odds-on favorite can lose the race even after plenty of rest and lots of training, and the underdog can come out of nowhere with a win. There are always mysterious factors involved. Nevertheless, winning horses—and winning men and women—have three things in common. Each of them needs to . . .

Start off on the right foot. The racing horse comes out of the gate on the right foot or with a "right stride." This sets the pace for an attitude of winning. The performance of the jockey is also, to a great extent, affected by the "right foot," or positive stance. The most dangerous position for a jockey is out in front. If he falls, he risks being trampled. Yet the jockey knows the only way to win is to be in the lead position, and that's where he wants to be.

The thrill of the race and the chance to parade in the winner's circle are motivation enough to put courage in the heart of both horse and rider. These rewards (along with a generous purse) outweigh the dangers and the obstacles.

Starting off on the right foot is vital to successful men and women too. A confident demeanor. A positive bearing. A courageous approach to life. These qualities can carry us well beyond our family heritage or our natural abilities.

Desire to be a winner. Both the winning jockey and the winning horse go into the race committed to finishing, regardless of position or circumstance. The burning desire to win never abates until the finish line is behind them because each one realizes that an ardent inner drive can give the final edge to an underdog.

In one of the most surprising upsets in recent horse racing, shocked fans watched as jockey Pat Day drove Lil E. Tee down the middle of the homestretch for a first-time win—after nine defeats.

I can certainly relate to Pat and Lil E. Tee's triumph. I was a slow starter myself. After poor grades in high school and a lifetime of low self-esteem, I was accepted into college on academic probation. My human spirit was deeply wounded, perhaps even broken, but I finally caught on to the excitement of learning. With the goal of a new life in front of me, I completed four years of college in two and a half years, graduating cum laude.

Even a slow starter can make a strong finish.

But as racetrack experts know, the secret to a winner's success is *on the inside.*

Be conditioned to endure. During the race Lil E. Tee won, an equally shocking event was the sight of the powerful French horse Arazi losing his action entirely at the 3/16 pole. Hailed by many as the "second coming of Secretariat," he gave a disappointing show. He began powerfully and continued with a lead midway through the final bend before completely losing stamina. The trainer's explanation was "too little preparation and conditioning. He just wasn't ready."

We all know Arazi people. They've got everything going for them—education, family support, and health. They expect to win and we believe they will, but something happens after a few successes. They begin to take winning for granted and learn the hard way:

> *Past victories aren't enough to carry*
> *you through the rest of your life.*

Although trainers speak of "breaking" horses, a horse's spirit is never actually broken; it is focused and fired into the task of running, finishing, and winning the race. Isn't the same true of people? Once, after I had spoken to a management team at the Chick-Fil-A Headquarters in Atlanta, a man walked up and handed me this note:

> *Success*
> *has nothing to do*
> *with fortune or fate.*
> *It has everything to do with passion.*

Whether or not you've made your way to Ocala, the race is on, and you're definitely a contender. So get ready! Get set! Now run with all you've got!

26 LAKELAND

Your Field of Dreams

A re we there yet? Are we there yet?" This was the ceaseless, aggravating cry of a little boy who thought three hours in the car was pure torture. Three hours is a short drive, you say? Not for this guy. I thought Mom only took me to see Granny and Granddad when she was mad at me, and my punishment was the long ride in the car.

One day, heading to Saint Cloud by way of US 27 I spotted an ad for the Detroit Tigers. They were in Lakeland for spring training. I had to get there! "Mom, Mom, pull over, pull over!"

I think Mom was so relieved to find anything at all that would keep my interest that she actually agreed to let me go see the baseball team play.

It's a day I'll never forget. There I was, *live* at Tigertown. I was watching my baseball heroes, listening to the roar of the crowd, absorbing the smell of "peanuts, popcorn, and Cracker Jacks." From then on, an intense love for baseball consumed me. I played ball from Little League to Babe Ruth in high school and in the American Legion League.

To top it all off, I was chosen to be bat boy for the Pittsburgh Pirates, who used to conduct their spring training at Terry Park in Fort Myers, just down the road from my house. These guys were my escape from family problems. They were the kind of men I wanted to be.

Like birds flying south for the winter, baseball teams migrate to Florida in February for spring training. It becomes one giant "Field of Dreams" as spectators cheer and fans stalk locker rooms for autographs or a glimpse of their favorite players. Spring training is the time and place for perfecting skills and teamwork, getting a head start on that September run for the World Series. Spring training involves . . .

Preparation. Today's athletes are expected to work out daily for conditioning and building strength during the off-season. This is the time to concentrate on timing and fundamentals. With the basics finely tuned, a player can handle any of life's "curve balls."

Practice. Continually working, improving, and learning are good habits with never-ending benefits. Technology is escalating at too rapid a pace for anyone to be satisfied with the status quo, especially when the status is nothing to "quo" about.

Proving. There comes a time when we have to prove what we're made of. It is said that character is what a person does when no one else is looking. Decisions, thoughts, reactions, and tendencies reveal the true, deep-down heart. Often, in the pursuit of a goal, we come to a fork in the road; difficulties, compromise, and setbacks confront us. Will we take the shortcut or blaze on through to the finish?

Pitching. Sell yourself. Believe in yourself. I have learned the hard way that if you do not think highly of yourself, it will soon be a unanimous feeling among peers. Nolan Ryan and the player who fails to make the team throw the same ball—the difference is in the delivery, the key to a good pitch.

Performance. If you take away all the excuses, the errors by others, and the obstacles everyone faces, what strides forward have you made? Can you check off any completed goals or milestones along the way? It's time to step up to the plate and *swing!*

At each of the baseball training camps, about fifty players are brought in, but only twenty-five will make it to the big leagues. Whether or not it's stated, the rule dealing with preparation, practice, proving, pitching, and performance is clear:

Focus until you finish
or
fizzle into failure.

As a young minister, I was greatly influenced by mentors, and I listened fondly to their tales. One story I'll never forget related the adventures of a hound-dog pup that was favored by the locals to become the region's greatest hunter.

After months of training, it was time to take the young hound on his first hunting trip. As he and his hunters traveled, a beautiful stag sauntered by, and the hound began the chase.

The men cheered, but only briefly. Soon a fox crossed the dog's path. Now nose-to-ground, following the fox, the dog continued his race—until he spotted a rabbit dashing under the brush.

This was too tempting a distraction for the young hound, and off he careened in the direction of the scurrying rabbit, who had already outwitted him.

Along the way, he accidentally flushed a covey of quail. What a spectacle that was! Dashing about in circles, the canine tried in vain to catapult himself in five different directions, only to find himself face-to-face with a field mouse.

Immediately he forgot the quail and chased the rodent into a hole.

When the exasperated owners finally caught up with the champion hound, they discovered a most pitiful sight. What had begun as a noble pursuit of a beautiful stag had ended with a panting, weary hound staring into a tiny mouse hole.

The moral of the story, and the message my mentor gave to me, I'll pass on to you:

"Young man, if you are going to achieve your potential to the fullest, stay focused on what you're going after and be sure to choose the most virtuous of pursuits."

Lakeland's baseball history offers lessons in patience, diligence, and tenacity. While all of life offers opportunities, the one who *finishes* the goal is the one who is crowned a winner.

Florida is the winter home for what is called "The Grapefruit League," consisting of twenty (at last count) professional teams. They play a thirty-game season beginning around the first of March and continuing through early April. Because information changes periodically it's best to call the Florida Sports Foundation office at 904-488-8347 to obtain a copy of the annual spring-training bulletin. In alphabetical order, the teams in the Grapefruit League are:

Atlanta Braves: Municipal Stadium, 715 Hank Aaron Drive, West Palm Beach, Florida 33401. Phone 407-683-6100.

Baltimore Orioles: Al Lang Stadium, 180 Second Avenue SE, Saint Petersburg, Florida 33701. Phone 813-923-1996.

Boston Red Sox: City of Palms Stadium, 2254 Edwards Drive, Fort Myers, Florida 33901. Phone 813-334-4700.

Chicago White Sox: Ed Smith Stadium, Twelfth Street and Tuttle Avenue, Sarasota, Florida 34237. Phone 813-954-4101.

Cincinnati Reds: Plant City Stadium, 1900 South Park Road, Plant City, Florida 33566. Phone 813-752-1878.

Cleveland Indians: Chain O'Lakes Stadium, Chain O'Lakes Park, Winter Haven, Florida. Phone 813-293-3900.

Detroit Tigers: Marchant Stadium, Tigertown, 1901 Lake Avenue, Lakeland, Florida 33802. Phone 813-686-8075.

Florida Marlins: Cocoa Expo, 500 Friday Road, Cocoa, Florida 32926. Phone 407-253-4433.

Houston Astros: Osceola County Stadium, 1000 Osceola Boulevard, Kissimmee, Florida 34744. Phone 407-933-6500.

Kansas City Royals: Baseball City Stadium, 300 Stadium Way, Davenport, Florida 34744. Phone 813-424-2500.

Los Angeles Dodgers: Holman Stadium, 4001 Twenty-sixth Street, Vero Beach, Florida 32961-2887. Phone 407-569-4900.

Minnesota Twins: Lee County Sports Complex 141000 Six Mile Cypress Parkway, Fort Myers, Florida 33912. Phone 813-768-4200.

Montreal Expos: Municipal Stadium, 715 Hank Aaron Drive, West Palm Beach, Florida 33401. Phone 407-684-6801.

New York Mets: Saint Lucie Stadium, 525 NW Peacock Boulevard, Port Saint Lucie, Florida 34986. Phone 497-871-2100.

New York Yankees: Fort Lauderdale Stadium, 5301 NW Twelfth Avenue, Fort Lauderdale, Florida 33309. Phone 305-776-1921.

Philadelphia Phillies: Jack Russell Memorial Stadium, 800 Phillies Drive, Clearwater, Florida 34615. Phone 813-441-9941.

Pittsburgh Pirates: McKechnie Field, Seventeenth Avenue West and Ninth Street West, Bradenton, Florida 34208. Phone 813-747-3031.

Saint Louis Cardinals: Al Lang Stadium, 180 Second Avenue, SE, Saint Petersburg, Florida 33701. Phone 813-896-4641.

Texas Rangers: Charlotte County Stadium, 2300 El Jobean Road, Port Charlotte, Florida 33948. Phone 813-625-9500.

Toronto Blue Jays: Dunedin Stadium at Grant Field, 311 Douglas Avenue, Dunedin, Florida 34698. Phone 813-733-9302.

P.S. If you're headed near Lakeland don't miss architect Frank Lloyd Wright's "Child of the Sun" collection, which is located on the campus of Florida Southern College. One of the most significant architects in American history, Wright came to Lakeland in 1938, and for more than twenty years he worked on the twelve structures, the largest architectural collection of its kind in the world.

27 JACKSONVILLE

Against All Odds

Driving through Jacksonville is an engineer's delight. Four hundred and forty-one bridges cobble together twenty miles of beaches and land like a puzzle to form "Florida's First Coast." How did a settlement once known as "Cowford" change itself into the international city of modern-day Jacksonville? I believe the secret of this city's success is its tenacity—against all odds—throughout its development.

Even nature attests to the fortitude of Jacksonville. The St. John's is the only American river to flow south to north. It was originally named *Illaka*, meaning "contrary," by the Timucuan Indians. Perhaps the strength of the river's current has been the silent mentor of the city in its triumph over adversity.

Wintering in the Jacksonville area, Harriet Beecher Stowe may have been moved by this river's defiant spirit when she wrote *Uncle Tom's Cabin.* The novel's grim portrayal of life under slavery was a major support to the antislavery cause. Published shortly before the Civil War, Stowe portrayed Tom as a pious, passive slave who was eventually beaten to death by his overseer, Simon Legree. Harriet chose to go against the popular point of view, daring to pen such a story for public reading.

In the early 1800s Jacksonville enjoyed a reputation as the county seat. Fine estates reigned along the river and in the back country. The lumber industry and cotton market flourished. Jacksonville's hotels and boarding houses were filled with visitors in search of a healthy climate.

Then came the Seminole War, several epidemics, two destructive fires, and a severe freeze that wiped out the fruit industry. With undiminished courage, the people overcame the tribulations, and by the time the War Between the States began, Jacksonville was already established as a thriving community.

Tourist travel and orange groves once again prospered, and Jacksonville became the focal point of many new endeavors. Then a sudden yellow fever epidemic descended upon the populace, leaving in its wake years of death and despair.

But yet again, Jacksonville turned the negative into positive with modified sanitation and general city improvements. Once more it fought back to a position of prosperity and status.

All seemed to be going well until Friday, May 3, 1901. In just eight hours an intense fire swiftly consumed 146 city blocks and 466 acres, destroying 2,368 buildings. The flare of the fire could be seen in Savannah, Georgia, and the plume of smoke was visible as far away as Raleigh, North Carolina.

With the characteristic spirit of Jacksonville, one business began to rebuild the very next day, and others soon followed. From that time on, with admirable determination, Jacksonville's citizens pushed against the odds, building and expanding through decades of history.

Today, Jacksonville is a thriving international trade seaport and business center with the largest state-of-the-art deep-water port in the South Atlantic. Not bad for a city originally known as the best spot to ford cows across the St. Johns River!

A festive, riverfront marketplace known as The Landings features a mile-long boardwalk and a potpourri of amusements, shops, and eateries. And in celebration of its inspiration through the ages, the river itself seems to say "Be proud of who you are. Dazzle the world with your uniqueness as you victoriously succeed against the odds."

Helen Keller echoed the spirit of Jacksonville when she wrote:

> *Life*
> *is either a daring adventure*
> *or nothing at all.*

In common usage, the word *daring* often implies a foolish, uncalculated risk. But in its truest form,

> **Daring describes a powerful**
> **combustion resulting from the**
> **blending of four fuels: fortitude,**
> **tenacity, determination, and faith.**

Fortitude describes John Foppe, a motivational speaker for the Zig Ziglar Corporation. It's a nice job, but not particularly noteworthy, until you consider that John was born with so many physical handicaps doctors gave him only one chance in a million to survive. They also claimed he would never walk. His other birth defects have been corrected or disappeared, but John still has no arms.

John describes his early years, saying, "I couldn't pop a pill and make the pain disappear. The permanency of my handicap faced me every day." Today John constantly travels across the country, using his feet like we use our hands, his toes in place of fingers, proclaiming the truth about attitude. Here are a few jewels from the crown of John Foppe:

"The rewards of being in competition with yourself are much deeper than those gained by competing with others."

"Nobody is perfect, so learn to forgive yourself for your own imperfections, making a clear distinction between self-confidence and self-esteem."

"I focus on what I have, rather than on what I don't have."

And here's my personal favorite:

"I came to the realization that our only real handicaps are those mental and emotional ones that prevent us from fully participating in life."

Tenacity brings to mind Olympic hopeful Gail Devers. She had tenacity when she narrowly won the women's one-hundred-meter race in the 1992 Summer Olympic Games. Sports commentators emphasized the two-and-a-half-inch spread and the one-hundredth-of-a-second difference in time between Gail and the runner-up, declaring it the closest sprint in the history of the Olympic Games. They called it nothing less than a miracle, and they weren't exaggerating.

In the three years before the race, Graves' Disease robbed Gail of her strength, her memory, the vision in one eye, even her hair. A sudden weight gain from 115 to 139 pounds, migraine headaches, and skin so sensitive it bled when she scratched it were listed among the catalog of symptoms she endured. In fact, at one time doctors seriously contemplated removing both of her feet. They told her she would never run again, and even the strength for long-distance walking was "against the odds."

Gail Devers refused to accept the diagnosis.

With the encouragement of her husband and the help of gold-medal Olympian Jackie Joyner-Kersee, she fought back against the impossible, one day at a time. No wonder *Newsweek* magazine titled her photo "Back from the Graves'."

Determination to finish the goal can be motive enough, even when there is no other reason to keep trying. As a five-year-old-boy, Glenn Cunningham suffered severe burns on his legs. Doctors told him he would never walk again, labeling him a hopeless cripple who would spend the rest of his days in a wheelchair.

When Glenn inquired of the recovery odds, the answer was a straightforward: "None."

Lying in bed, unable to move his thin, scar-covered legs, Glenn thought about the odds and then made a decision: "Next week, I'm going to get out of bed. I'm going to walk."

His mother tells the story of watching him through the window as he exercised in the yard. By pulling up on the handles of an old plow, Cunningham forced his twisted legs to move. Then, enduring excruciating pain, he learned to take one step, then another and another until he really was walking.

It was an astonishing conquest. But it wasn't enough for Glenn. He decided to try running.

Each achievement fueled his determination, and next he told his family and friends, "I always believed that I could walk again, and I did. Now I'm going to run faster than anybody has ever run." Foolish talk for a crippled boy, even for one who forced his body to walk through grueling repetitive exercise.

Or was it?

Cunningham became a great mile runner who set the world's record of 4:06.8 in 1934. He was honored as the outstanding athlete of the century at Madison Square Garden. "No pain, no gain" takes on new meaning with the story of Glenn Cunningham.

Faith in your future, combined with determination, can take you where you want to go. First Baptist Church of Jacksonville knows all about faith. When I first heard of the church's new building program, I wondered, *Hasn't anyone explained to them about the death of downtown churches? About the traffic and the distances most people have to drive to get there?*

If they'd heard that report, it didn't matter to them. Today "the miracle of downtown Jacksonville" has moved into a brand-new nine-thousand-seat, 18.5-million-dollar auditorium. With two and half miles of pews and fifty-four doors, the building is free of all debt. First Baptist Church has shown a pattern of being willing to go against the current and fight the flow.

No one believed two pastors could co-exist as equal leaders, but under the dynamic co-leadership of Dr. Jerry Vines and Dr. Homer Lindsay, Jr., this amazing church continues to grow. They still believe that old-time religion and values work in modern American families, and more than twenty-two thousand dedicated church members prove they're right. These incredibly friendly people have as their motto, "First Baptist of Jacksonville is the church of the open door."

Thinking about Jacksonville's tenacity and those four extraordinary success stories, it's become clear to me: There are people aplenty who can achieve the ordinary, the possible. But it's the few, the very few, who have the *fortitude, tenacity, determination,* and *faith* to accomplish the impossible. And they are the ones who know the reward of overcoming the odds. Robert Louis Stevenson once declared:

Life
ought to be dashingly used
and cheerfully hazardous.

Perhaps it could be said in briefer terms, more suited to our contemporary language:

Go for it!

28 SAINT AUGUSTINE

Backyard Riches, Front-Yard Dreams

St. Augustine, Florida, is America's oldest city. A stroll down the vintage streets of the Spanish Quarter is like a trip back through history. The authenticity of the costumed artisans and careful attention to details completely remove the tourist from the twentieth century.

Watch as skilled artisans weave lambs' fleece into a square of wool, fashion a broom from pieces of straw, and forge tools out of scraps of iron over red-hot coals. Elsewhere in Saint Augustine you can walk into the country's oldest schoolhouse. Peer through the bars of the oldest jail. Or visit an authentic Spanish fort. Your visit will carry you through four centuries.

Next, climb hills to lookout posts, examine original cannons, or wander through tropical forests in search of the Fountain of Youth. I went searching for it with all the vigor of an explorer, hoping to find the clue Ponce de Leon had perhaps missed. What I found was a park, built in memory of the brave explorer.

At first the memorial seemed odd to me. After all, Ponce de Leon had failed in his quest. Then I realized that the memorial is not in honor of de Leon's discovery; instead it was built out of respect for his courageous and brave persona, his spirit of adventure, and his abandonment of all that is sure.

True, he found no Fountain of Youth, but he discovered a land of unbridled beauty and opportunity. *La Florida,* Ponce de Leon called it, meaning "feast of flowers"; the name was later shortened to Florida. Setting out to prove he could do the impossible, he taught us all a lesson:

Be open to a boundless variety of possibilities.

So many of us set out with enthusiasm on our personal quest, only to find disappointment awaiting us. A rumored "pot of gold" at the end of the rainbow is a powerful motivator. But what most people haven't discovered is that the rainbow is actually a complete circle. I think this proves that . . .

Whatever you're yearning for
might very well be found
in your own front yard!

Scientists tell us that two people, standing side by side in admiration of a rainbow, are actually seeing light refracted and reflected by different sets of raindrops. Just as each person has a future that is molded and shaped by unique experiences, sorrows, talents, and abilities, each of us has a personal rainbow. And it may not be as far out of reach as we think.

Author Russell H. Conwell relates the intriguing story of Ali Hafed in his book, *Acres of Diamonds.* As an old Arab guide remembers it, Hafed was fascinated by the idea of immense wealth. Leaving behind family and friends, he embarked on a journey around the world in search of a diamond mine. He gave up success as a Persian farmer, sure that vast treasure was always just around the corner. Instead, he found starvation and despair. Ultimately, he cast himself into a foaming, briny sea, never to rise in this life again.

In the meantime, the new owner of Hafed's farm set to work plowing and planting. One day, working with his hands in the soil, he came upon a black stone. Holding it up for closer inspection, the farmer noticed it reflected the hues of the rainbow. Thinking it quite pretty, he cleaned it and placed it on the mantel as an ornament.

A friend noticed the stone one day and exclaimed, "Has Hafed returned? Did he finally find his diamonds?"

"Oh no," the farmer explained, "that's only a stone from the backyard."

The visitor adamantly declared that the stone was of immense value. Together the astonished farmer and his friend searched the backyard, uncovering hundreds of the stones, which actually were priceless diamonds. The once-abandoned farm turned out to be the most magnificent diamond mine in all the world. Reportedly, many of the crown jewels of Russia and England were mined there.

If Hafed had believed he could achieve success right where he was, he would have left behind an entirely different life story.

I meet people every day who live in contingency and anticipation of the next coming event in their lives. The words *if* and *when* pepper their language as thickly as spice in a bowl of Cajun red beans and rice. But what about today? What about the here and now?

Ali Hafed was already wealthy—right where he was. He just failed to recognize it.

Ponce de Leon learned that no matter what the discovery, *success is yours—right now—if you'll make the most of what you've found.*

Here's some essential daily self-talk. Tell yourself every morning,

I can do it!
I can do it where I am!
I can do it where I am right now.

I can do it. My oldest daughter, Melissa, is hearing-impaired, but she loves music and enjoys singing. She came to me recently with a startling announcement. "Dad," she said, "I'm going to sing a solo at church."

I really didn't know what to say. I didn't want to discourage her, but I wasn't sure if I should encourage her either. After all, a hearing-impaired singer might not be exactly on pitch.

"Do you think you're ready, honey?" I queried.

"Dad, I've been practicing in my room and in the backyard for years. I can do this."

Melissa not only sang, she sang well! And what she may have lacked in melody, she made up for with enthusiasm. I learned a valuable lesson from her as I watched and listened.

Transform that ongoing rehearsal
in the theater of your mind
into an actual performance
on the stage of life.
It's showtime!

I can do it right where I am. Sam Walton visualized a store where middle-income America could shop economically. He then made the dream come true from his home town of Bentonville, Arkansas. Today Wal-Marts are synonymous with good merchandise at a fair price, and they can be seen all across America.

J. B. Hunt's yellow trucks are visible on virtually any American highway, transporting goods from one coast to the other. Just down the road from Bentonville in the small town of Springdale, Arkansas, Hunt's business has a reputation for dependability and efficiency.

For both of these small-town companies, the dream of expansion into the "front yard" resulted in multimillion-dollar profits. And even today, their headquarters remain in their "backyards."

> *While you're waiting to move*
> *to a better job*
> *or another opportunity,*
> *make the most of everything today offers.*
> *You may surprise yourself!*

I can do it right where I am right now. After speaking at conferences, I enjoy meeting people and swapping stories. Often a man or women will speak to me about a goal or dream. Usually, they finish with a disclaimer about the reason they can't "go for it" right now.

Sometimes I hear, "By the time I spend three years at school, I'll be forty . . . fifty . . . or sixty years old!"

My reply is: "In three years you'll be forty . . . fifty . . . sixty . . . anyway, won't you?"

Others say, "It's just not a good time for me to start right now."

I have to say, "Do you know when your 'good time' *will* be here? After all, the sooner you begin, the closer you are to finishing."

There's a lesson to be learned from Ponce de Leon's wonderful discovery of *La Florida*. And don't fail to remember poor old Hafed's diamond-studded fields, left behind in his desperate search for riches. Look at it this way:

> *There is no better place or time*
> *to make your rainbow*
> *of dreams come true*
> *than HERE and NOW!*

29 PENSACOLA

Soaring Above and Beyond

Off they go! The jets streak by so swiftly there is no chance of predicting their direction. Only the wisps of white behind them leave a sure mark of where they have been. Above pristine, white-sand beaches, they fly in precise formation with such power and force that the very sky seems to quake. Claiming the heavens as their own, these are the Blue Angels, elite ambassadors of the U.S. Navy and Marine Corps aviators who serve America.

Beneath the jets' formation lies the city of Pensacola, with one of the most historical districts in the United States. The city's long history spans four centuries, creating an alluring tapestry of dreams, disappointments, and determination; of pioneers, patriots, and prisoners. Names like Geronimo and Andrew Jackson are but a few.

Today Pensacola stands confidently fulfilling her destiny as a defender of freedom. Home to aircraft carriers and battleships, the U.S. Naval Aviation Museum, the Pensacola Naval Supply Center, and the Pensacola Naval Air Station, she is nicknamed "the Mother-in-law of the Navy." No wonder America's beloved Blue Angels are based here.

The Blue Angels are tactical jet pilots, staff officers, and transport pilots who have demonstrated superior abilities as naval officers and aviators. Each one has completed a minimum of fifteen hundred tactical jet hours, has done a tour of duty aboard an aircraft carrier, and is a career officer. At any given time, there are as many as one hundred applicants for any available Blue Angel position.

Having the opportunity to take a close look at this elite troop of aviators, my curiosity was piqued. What could men of such dedication and intensity teach the rest of us about successful soaring? Here are some valuable truths I learned from their commander:

You don't soar "above and beyond" overnight. These difficult and demanding jobs are learned a little at a time. At the beginning, there is a necessary mastery of the basics.

Soaring above and beyond is eventually accomplished by a willingness to reach beyond minimum requirements.

Practice is a necessary daily habit in the quest for precision. By the time they fly their first demonstration, the Blue Angel pilots have flown in more than 120 rehearsal shows, and they have been flying twice a day, Monday through Saturday, during winter training. Show precision is achieved through repetition.

Do it
until you get it right.
Then do it
a hundred times more.

Expect the unexpected. These world-class pilots realize that they must be able to face a variety of problems or situations at split-second notice. They have learned the essential requirement of exercising control over their circumstances, and they are on the constant alert for any eventuality.

When I asked the commander to give me a personal example of a surprising twist in flight, he didn't hesitate to offer this account. "Flying the lead plane in a show, I felt a sudden thump to the plane's tail. Thinking I had been bumped by another plane, I struggled to keep in line, knowing the formation of the other planes was dependent on me. Hours later at the debriefing, I learned of the danger the pilot just behind me had experienced.

"What I had interpreted as a thump was actually turbulence created by the thrust of a sudden change in his flight pattern. It seems his throttle froze in mid-flight, leaving the pilot to make an instantaneous decision. There was only one choice—to fly straight up and out of the pattern to keep from endangering those around him. He was able to rectify and recover the situation because he was prepared to expect the unexpected. But for both of us, the available reaction time was only seconds."

Teamwork is essential to the goal. The Blue Angels are highly dedicated, multi-talented individuals, all of whom would be labeled "Type A" personalities. Yet they personify teamwork from the ground up. Flying at speeds of approximately four hundred miles per hour with only three feet between their aircraft, these men must have complete confidence in each other. They call it "unqualified faith" in their fellow flyers.

If at any time a pilot becomes undependable in his calculated moves, he loses credibility with the team. The slightest careless move spells danger to the others. Such grave responsibility at first seems overwhelming. But then it struck me—the same principle holds true for all of us, every day, in every reaction and decision we make.

*The final product of any organization is a direct reflection
of the amount of teamwork executed in its production.*

As team members work together, they build mutual trust.

Every flight has to be your best. It takes the tireless dedication of each squadron member to pull off a synchronized show at such amazing speeds. Besides the excitement and challenge, this particular career choice offers dual honors: to represent the freedom and power of the United States and to remind the public of the dedication of Navy and Marine Corps officers.

The quest for the best is discussed at length in preflight meetings. Conducted before every flight, a representative of each department, from maintenance to administration, is required to attend these meetings. During this time, contingency plans are discussed regarding everything from weather changes to air traffic, from tower obstructions to birds, from frequency problems to mechanical failure. The men are grilled again and again about handling any conceivable scenario.

The quest for perfection does not end there. Each flight is video-taped, and post-flight meetings last for hours as discussions address strengths and weaknesses of individuals and divisions. Every move is scrutinized, and the question is always before them: "Could we have done better in any area?"

Unseen labors produce visible accomplishments. "Without the guys on the ground we couldn't do what we do in the air," one pilot told me. Little wonder the maintenance troops are at work by 5:30 A.M. fueling and inspecting the jets. After a run, they top off the tanks, and clean the jets for the next flight. They recover the jets and do a turnaround inspection twice a day, repairing when necessary. The jets are then cleaned again after the last flight.

The crews work as long as necessary, sometimes long into the night, to be ready for the next morning's flight. They may never be approached by an autograph seeker, but everyone agrees they share equally in the fame and accomplishment.

In fact, it takes eighty-five people working around the clock and behind the scenes in order for six pilots to perform a show. What happens in the hangar determines, to a great degree, what happens in the heavens.

Stephen R. Covey calls this "the essence of character growth:

> *Private victories*
> *precede public victories."*

Successful people are willing to do whatever it takes to accomplish the goal. Each member of the team must be willing to do his or her share and more. Cross-training gives team members an edge of awareness about the total operation. This enables them to spot problems and handle a variety of situations on the road.

These navy personnel are highly motivated individuals. Their primary objective is to be extremely successful in their endeavors, even if it means working behind the scenes.

I asked the commander of the Blue Angels exactly what it is that sets one applicant apart from another. If all are required to have the same training and qualifications, how would he select the few from the many?

He replied, "We look for many qualities that cannot be taught or learned. Each pilot must exude a personality of confidence, strength, and sensitivity. A positive attitude, a willingness to learn, and a desire to go beyond the routine to get the job done are essential."

I left my Blue Angels encounter feeling full of patriotism and respect for these men of valor and dedication. Their example ignited a recommitment in me to reach beyond the norm in the spirit of excellence.

As Dr. Tim LaHaye wrote (and as the Blue Angels personify):

> *The future belongs to those*
> *who are prepared for it*
> *educationally, relationally,*
> *vocationally, and spiritually.*

30 THE EMERALD COAST

Louder Isn't Always Better

W hether I'm hungry or not, I head for the Back Porch restaurant in Destin any time I'm within an hour of it. The food is great, but the view is spectacular. Emerald-green water, sugar-white sand, and roaring surf provide the perfect background for a leisurely dinner.

Destin and Fort Walton comprise Florida's "Emerald Coast," and their beaches consistently rate in the top five in the world. As a young man I admired them. Now, after traveling to more than forty countries, I have seen nothing to rival them.

These crown jewels of Florida are the most accessible beaches to the rest of the country, yet they are the least known. I can almost offer you a money-back guarantee that any time of the year you'll find an uncrowded stretch of beach or a desolate sand dune. More than a hundred miles of clean, fine sand stretch across the Panhandle, yet you won't find a major ad campaign promoting the area. Tourism along the Emerald Coast relies on the strength of a good reputation. Its residents firmly believe you don't have to be the loudest to be the best. As Great Britain's former prime minister Margaret Thatcher once said,

> *Being great*
> *is like being a lady.*
> *If you have to tell people you are,*
> *you aren't.*

Phrases such as "toot your own horn" and "look out for number one" have become quite popular. Somewhere along the line, style began to win out over substance. To quote historian Warren Susman: "The nineteenth century was the age of character, but the twentieth is an age of personality."

The character of meekness may be perceived as weakness, but it actually requires a great deal of strength. It is a controlled desire to see others do well, and it literally means an absence of pretense. When you watch the mammoth killer whale Shamu obey a one-hundred-pound trainer at Sea World, you see meekness—power willingly under control.

When a person shouts "Look at me!" he or she had better be ready for the ensuing examination. Abraham Lincoln used an obvious metaphor:

> *What kills a skunk*
> *is the publicity it gives itself.*

Or consider this advice from Socrates:

> *The way to gain a good reputation*
> *is to endeavor to be*
> *what you desire to appear.*

A person becomes known by his or her words, deeds, and reactions, and no one will ever be wealthy enough to be able to buy back his or her past. A slip in character can take years or even a lifetime to repair.

I read with sadness about a congressman who was publicly accused of impropriety. He endured a media smear against his good name and a lengthy, well-broadcast trial before he was cleared of the charges. Six months of probing humiliation was summarized in a moment of announcement: "Acquitted."

The accusation proved false; however, the damage to his character was irrevocable.

Exiting the courtroom the last day, he was approached by several members of the press requesting a final statement. He replied with a terse inquiry: "To what room can I go to regain the reputation you have taken from me?"

**It is far easier
to keep a reputation
than to ever regain it.**

Without depending solely on self-promotion, the Emerald Coast has earned—and kept—a wonderful reputation. It has done so primarily by being true to its own best qualities. Maybe it translates for us like this: Be yourself. Be the best you can be. And before long, everyone will notice how very exceptional you are!

True success is not measured against the achievements of others. Remember, *you can be a peacock one day and a feather duster the next!*

Success is synonymous with excellence.

Success is performing my personal best consistently.

Success is not climbing over anyone else on my way up the ladder, but helping others climb as I go.

Most importantly,

Success is winning in the competition against myself.

31 | SHARKS

"Swimming" with Difficult People

Efficient killing machine," "scavenger of the ocean," "enemy of the sea." You know what I'm talking about . . . *sharks!* These are but a few of the terrible names given to the marvelous and mysterious shark.

After a trilogy of *Jaws* movies, an undercurrent of fear lingers in the minds of anyone approaching Florida beaches for the first time. In actual fact, this fear simply isn't necessary. Experts tell us that our chances of experiencing an unprovoked shark attack while swimming in Florida waters are one in 100 million. Driving the freeway to work is much more dangerous. This "evil menace" is actually a beneficial contributor to science and medicine, and the list of the shark's positive offerings to mankind is amazing.

Television commercials have told us for years about the value of shark oil in skin creams, burn patients often rely on shark cartilage for skin grafting, and sharks have given science a great deal of information about human kidney function. Researchers continue to be amazed by sharks' resistance to cancer, and they hope to unlock keys to cancer prevention through their studies.

More than three hundred shark species have been identified, but we'll concentrate on those familiar to Florida waters. Of course, in our American culture, we've all heard the jokes about the predatory and aggressive "sharks" inhabiting the waters of our everyday lives. You'll soon see that the real ocean-dwelling creatures share certain peculiarities with the difficult people we know, live with, and work with. See if you recognize any of these characters.

Spinner shark. A long snout and small eyes distinguish the spinner. He may remind you of someone whose nose is in everyone else's business and whose limited vision sees only what he or she wants to see. Human spinners thrive on gossip and "Well, I heard . . . ," and every word you say to them can be used against you later.

Lemon shark. With two dorsal fins, the lemon reminds me of the negative person. All of life is a "lemon" to him or her, and their first word or thought is either a complaint or an excuse.

The two dorsal fins are also symbolic of the "double-minded" souls who can't stick with an idea or a conviction. These folks are easily swayed and distracted, often going with the popular vote. You can usually count on them to agree with whatever person they talked to last. Can you relate so far?

Mako shark. The mako has a spindled body and pointed snout, is fast-moving, and has blade-like teeth. This represents the quick and deep-cutting criticism of someone who speaks carelessly and moves quickly, instinctively going for the throat.

As difficult as it may seem, these insults shouldn't be taken personally. The person doing the criticizing is the one with the problem—his or her nature is bloodthirsty, just like a shark's.

Nurse shark. The nurse shark's dorsal fins are set far back; it is slow-moving and likes to dwell on the bottom of the ocean. Nurse sharks depict the depressed co-worker or family member who is always running behind and feels overwhelmed. These men and women are melancholy, and their only real goal seems to be making you feel despondent too. Keep your attitude and mood safe from these "nurses."

Bull shark. The bull shark has a short, blunt head and rough skin. This reminds me of the opinionated person with little patience for anyone else's point of view. A stormy reaction will result if you don't happen to see things his or her way.

Blacknose shark. The small, gray blacknose is easily identified by a black spot on the snout. You know this kind—that "black spot" of the past is tattooed on the spirit so deeply that contentment in the present or excitement about the future are unattainable.

As a result, every new day is measured against the failure and hurt of yesterday. These unhappy souls see themselves as constant victims of circumstance.

Tiger shark. Large-mouthed and broad-headed, the tiger shark is well known as an attacker. In the human aquarium, these people are known as "big mouths." They have no control over their temperament or words, attacking and destroying as they go. A single strike from one of these sharks can devastate even the most positive person.

Brown (sandbar) shark. An active swimmer, the brown shark can travel a considerable distance; it ventures into seasonal migrations. This person's moods swing up and down like the waves. No one really knows what territory those moods will cover from one day to the next or whether he or she can be depended on to finish the job. Things are always "probably better" somewhere other than where he or she is at the moment.

Most sharks, like most people, are harmless. Even so, personalities and leadership styles can clash. When this happens, a little extra navigational preparation can expedite your swim through the channels of family, friendship, and career. I read with interest the article entitled "Swimmers Can Minimize the Risk of Attack" in *The Florida Survival Handbook*. It echoed practical advice for the workplace:

Stay in groups. Avoid one-on-one situations with a difficult individual if at all possible. When a discussion or meeting is necessary, take along a third party or involve several people who might be working on the project. This minimizes the chance of personal attack.

Do not wander too far from shore. Stay on the subject at hand and continually come back to the goal. Personal views are better left undiscussed as you stay focused on the main issues, not on the individuals around you. When a shark tries to sidetrack you with criticism, depression, or negative words, just keep swimming mentally toward your goal.

Avoid the water during darkness. If you sense a shark is experiencing a period of stress or moodiness, stay away until a more opportune time. Or try to create an alternate atmosphere. When a person is agitated, a strike on someone else is almost inevitable.

Do not enter the water if you are bleeding. Don't set yourself up by being unprepared, emotionally overcharged, or physically exhausted. One basic rule stays with me: Don't make a decision when you are tired. You want to meet the "shark" with the advantages of inner strength and organization in your corner.

Do not wear shiny jewelry in the water. Many difficult people are intensely jealous or greedy. Don't provoke either of these characteristics by boasting or by intentionally making yourself look good in front of others. Your own accomplishments speak volumes, and you don't need to open your mouth. What you've successfully completed cannot be refuted or denied. Giving co-workers an opportunity to speak your praises rather than doing it yourself works toward a team spirit of appreciation for one another.

Avoid waters with known effluents or sewage. If you know that a certain phrase or situation will automatically bring out the worst in the person, run from it. Make mental or even written notes evaluating a flareup in an effort to avert a future disaster.

A porpoise sighting does not indicate the absence of sharks. When the waters look friendly and calm, consider a "worst-case" scenario. Always be prepared to give a clear, concise answer in the event of questioning, thus keeping your personal feelings from interfering. Impromptu answers can be held against you later. And "I didn't mean it that way" makes you appear to be an ineffective communicator.

Use extra caution when waters are murky. Be sure you are specifically informed as to what is expected of you and when it is to be completed. Keep a clear focus on what you are trying to accomplish and a firm comprehension of your job description. "I didn't understand" is a lame excuse for an intelligent person like you.

Refrain from excess splashing. Nothing draws fire more quickly than excuses. Keep your responses concise and simple and don't pass the buck. Accept the responsibility for error and solve the problem quickly. Thrashing about is a sure attraction for attack.

Exercise caution near steep drop-offs. When you sense contention brewing, back off. If you are stubbornly persistent you might win the battle but lose the war. Don't try to get even by making the "bad guy" look inferior, no matter how easy it is. Concentrate on an attitude of excellence and the obvious comparison will result in a potent image for you.

Do not enter an area where sharks are known to be present. Do whatever is necessary to surround yourself with positive, competent people, and work toward possessing the qualities you personally look for in leadership. Beware of adopting the characteristics of the sharks swimming nearby. Go for the grace of the dolphin instead.

Do not harass a shark. You can't win in a fight against a shark, and a truly difficult person will never concede defeat, no matter how the reality is presented. Arguments result in words better left unsaid and harsh feelings not easily forgotten. Put that same energy into doing a superior job and allow the satisfaction of a job well done to be your victory.

I have added one cautionary note of my own: **When you see a fin, identify it!** While deep-sea fishing, it's not uncommon to see a fin here and there in the water. The only way to tell if it's a shark or a dolphin is to keep watching. If it's constant and consistent, it warns of the danger of a shark. If it only occasionally surfaces, it's a harmless dolphin.

In the same way, be aware of bad habits that stay around too long—things like an uncontrolled temper, procrastination, flirtation, a bad attitude, blaming others. If it's a shark habit, swim away from it. If you think it's a dolphin habit, keep an eye on it just in case.

Oddly enough, this feared creature has given us many benefits—delicious meat as well as beautiful personal and decorative items to be enjoyed. While the risk of shark attack is minimal, the benefits of the shark are incredible.

Difficult people may have the same kind of value. If we are wise we can keep them from harming us. We can learn a great deal about destructive attitudes and bad habits from observing them. And they may have hidden positive qualities that will make valuable contribution to our lives and even our careers—once we learn how to deal safely with them.

32 THE GREATEST LESSON OF ALL

I hope you've enjoyed this compilation of thoughts and ideas that I've gathered over the years in sunny Florida. I have certainly found delight in reviewing my scrapbook of lessons, contemplating them, and sharing them with you. I have just one more lesson to offer you, and as they say, I have saved the best for last.

The most powerful things I've ever learned were not taught to me in Florida's brilliant sunshine, but in the shade of Granddad's huge orange-grove trees in the little town of St. Cloud, Florida. Though he was stooped with age, he stood taller than any other man in my life. In my eyes, Granddad towered over the superstar athletes I met as a bat boy during spring training, outshone any of the astronauts from NASA, and certainly outclassed any of the loud, flashy stepdads who blew through my life like some fickle wind.

During my personal hurricanes of hurt, Granddad was the eye of the storm. In my parents' world of "fatal attractions," it was Granny and Granddad, married for more than sixty years, that I looked to, hoping to discover the reality of genuine, faithful love. I don't recall any inspirational speeches or amazing expressions of wisdom from Granddad. Instead, he taught me through his everyday life how to be a man of character.

Even working in my grandfather's garden with him provided me with the kind of basic instructions every kid should cherish. "Hoe to the end of the row, Jay," he'd tell me. "Always finish what you start."

Year after year, I watched Granddad face life's blows without the need of alcohol or drugs. What a rare strength he displayed, so foreign to my experience and environment.

My grandfather told me, for example, never to judge people by the color of their skin, but by what was inside.

He reminded me that character is keeping your end of the bargain even when the original circumstances of the agreement change. I saw this not only in his business, but in our family life as well. My grandparents raised my older half-brother, Rocky, as their own son and gave him the stability of a loving home.

As far as Rocky and I were concerned, Granddad cast the longest shadow of any man we ever met.

He used to tell me about Florida's sinkholes. Famous for swallowing up shopping centers, homes, and miles of land, sinkholes are collapsed caverns that were created underneath the surface of the earth through erosion of stone and soil. Granddad said that sinkholes are a lesson to mankind about the importance of building our lives on a sure foundation.

He explained to me that two basic types of damage are caused by sinkholes. A sinkhole can slowly erode the support of a home, causing the foundation to shift and crack. Or it can suddenly open up and swallow the entire structure, causing total destruction. When news of sinkhole destruction hits, residents in the surrounding areas become fearful, feeling they can no longer trust the ground they walk on.

There are those whose lives are similar to a Florida sinkhole: Everything looks great on the exterior, but underneath the support structure is deteriorating dangerously. A great restlessness shifts under the surface.

Sad to say, that was an apt description of my own life. The occasional stability Granddad gave me was eroded and ravaged by everyday realities. Broken homes, alcoholic stepdads, abuse, and loneliness drove me into the very life I had hated since boyhood—drugs and drinking. Predictably, my entire foundation collapsed, and I found myself in a sinkhole, desperately searching for rescue and a way to rebuild.

At seventeen, I had already tried almost everything in the way of the bottle, pills, or cheap thrills to find happiness. When a school friend started talking to me about the "basics of life" I remembered Granddad, and I found myself feeling cautiously optimistic.

My friend told me about a man named Matthew who had once been ruled by a passion for money and self-gratification. After a radical realignment of his priorities, Matthew had learned to live under the authority of a new edict—the Golden Rule and the Sermon on the Mount. "Read it for yourself, Jay, and see," he challenged me, offering a Bible.

What began half-heartedly soon intrigued me. "Could this be truth?" I pondered the possibilities of Matthew 6:33:

> ***Seek first***
> ***the kingdom of God***
> ***and His righteousness,***
> ***and all these things***
> ***shall be added to you.***

The words jumped off the page. For me, the word *things* meant peace of mind, and peace was the foundation I longed to build my life upon.

That night I prayed a simple prayer: "God, here is my life. I know I've messed it up, but if You'll give me a chance to start over again, I'm willing to try." There was no visible change. I saw no angels and no blinding lights. But a peace pervaded my soul and lifted me into a new vision of the future.

Don't ask me why—no one told me to do it—but the very next thing I did was to flush my drugs and booze down the commode. (The rats in the sewer were high for weeks!) Next morning I picked up the Bible and started to read. I found myself getting back to the basics, rearranging my priorities, and enjoying a life of simple faith.

You have already read about the restoration between my dad and me, but something else from my past was "added to me" a few years ago. I had just flown in to be with mother for what was to be the last time. She had battled cancer for many years, and I walked into Orlando Regional Medical Center grieving and remembering. Hearing a page for "Mr. Strack," I fearfully and promptly responded, only to be told the page was for "the" Mr. Strack, the CEO of the hospital.

Just then I turned as an unfamiliar man asked, "Are you Jay?"

I nodded my head, still expecting grievous news, when he said, "I'm your brother Gary."

"Look, I like a joke as much as anybody, but not today," I replied in disbelief and exhaustion. "My mom is dying. This just isn't funny right now."

Gary proceeded to tell me my mom's name, my dad's name, and some very personal facts from my childhood. When he was done, I knew he was telling the truth. No one had ever told me about my dad's former marriage or his son Gary. At the age of thirty, I met him for the first time. Over the last decade Gary and I have been together often, and I must tell you he is one of the most visionary leaders I have ever met in my life. In his years as CEO of Orlando Regional Medical Center, he has helped expand the hospital to include the Arnold Palmer Hospital for Children and Women as well as the Orlando Cancer Center. The brother I never knew has become my respected mentor and adviser. I told you the city of Orlando means "magic" to me!

Now, after more than twenty years (I'll never tell how many more), I can tell you I have no interest in ever turning back to my old life. My Bible tells me that God sees my year from the beginning to the end, and I depend on His presence as I plan to live each day to the fullest. For me, the ultimate definition of success is to seek first the kingdom of God, for I know by personal experience that all the rest will then be added.

So, there it is! I don't know everything, but this much I am sure of: Everything worth knowing I learned growing up in Florida. That is . . . until I moved to Texas!